GW01271920

FL

by Charlie Josephine

∥SAMUEL FRENCH∥

ISBN 978-0-573-01341-6

concordtheatricals.co.uk
concordtheatricals.com

FOR AMATEUR PRODUCTION ENQUIRIES

UNITED KINGDOM AND WORLD
EXCLUDING NORTH AMERICA
licensing@concordtheatricals.co.uk
020-7054-7298

Each title is subject to availability from Concord Theatricals, depending upon country of performance.

This work is published by Samuel French, an imprint of Concord Theatricals Ltd.

The Professional Rights in this play are controlled by The Agency (London) Ltd., 24 Pottery Ln, London W11 4LZ.

written permission of the publisher. No one shall share this title, or part of this title, to any social media or file hosting websites.

The moral right of Charlie Josephine to be identified as author of this work has been asserted in accordance with Section 77 of the Copyright, Designs and Patents Act 1988.

USE OF COPYRIGHTED MUSIC

A licence issued by Concord Theatricals to perform this play does not include permission to use the incidental music specified in this publication. In the United Kingdom: Where the place of performance is already licensed by the PERFORMING RIGHT SOCIETY (PRS) a return of the music used must be made to them. If the place of performance is not so licensed then application should be made to PRS for Music (www.prsformusic.com). A separate and additional licence from PHONOGRAPHIC PERFORMANCE LTD (www.ppluk.com) may be needed whenever commercial recordings are used. Outside the United Kingdom: Please contact the appropriate music licensing authority in your territory for the rights to any incidental music.

USE OF COPYRIGHTED THIRD-PARTY MATERIALS

Licensees are solely responsible for obtaining formal written permission from copyright owners to use copyrighted third-party materials (e.g., artworks, logos) in the performance of this play and are strongly cautioned to do so. If no such permission is obtained by the licensee, then the licensee must use only original materials that the licensee owns and controls. Licensees are solely responsible and liable for clearances of all third-party copyrighted materials, and shall indemnify the copyright owners of the play(s) and their licensing agent, Concord Theatricals Ltd., against any costs, expenses, losses and liabilities arising from the use of such copyrighted third-party materials by licensees.

IMPORTANT BILLING AND CREDIT REQUIREMENTS

If you have obtained performance rights to this title, please refer to your licensing agreement for important billing and credit requirements.

Boundless Theatre and Shoreditch Town Hall

Flies

by Charlie Josephine

Flies received its first performance in London at
Shoreditch Town Hall on 22 February 2023

Flies

by Charlie Josephine

Cast

Girl 1	Willow Traynor
Girl 2	Rosa Amos
Girl 3	Annabel Gray
Girl 4	Louisa Hamdi
Girl 5	Pearl Adams
Girl 6	Afriya-Jasmine Nylander
Girl 7	Ellie Rose Amit

Creative Team

Writer	Charlie Josephine
Director	Julia Head
Designer	Cat Fuller
Movement Director	Nandi Bhebhe
Lighting Designer	Martha Godfrey
Sound Designer	Nicole Raymond
AV Desginer	James Kent
Production Manager	Misha Mah
Stage Manager	Adriana Perucca
Assistant Stage Manager	Katie Glassbrook
Assistant Director	Elizabeth Anderson

Flies is supported by Cockayne - Grant for the Arts and The London Community Foundation

Boundless Theatre and Shoreditch Town Hall wish to thank the following for their help with the production: Sarah Goodall and all at The BRIT School, Stevie Raine, Xana, Elayce Ismail, Bryony Shanahan, Erica Wyman and James Pidgeon

The Cast

Willow Traynor
Willow trained at The BRIT School on the Musical Theatre course. This included The Bridge Company course. Flies is Willow's Professional Debut.

Training credits: Cases, Meat and Dance Like Nobody Is Watching (Except Everyone Is).

Rosa Amos
Rosa trained at The BRIT School including The Bridge Company course. Flies is Rosa's Professional Debut.

Rosa is now part of The Almeida Theatres Young Company and will be Performing in Rush.

Training credits: The Welkin, The Winter's Tale and A Doll's House.

Annabel Gray
Annabel trained at The BRIT School on the Post 16 Theatre Course. This included The Bridge Company course. Flies is Annabel's Professional Debut.

Bridge Company Credits: Little Lights devised by the company, directed by Liz Bacon.

Training credits: The Welkin, Macbeth and Cathy.

Louisa Hamdi
Louisa trained at The BRIT School. Flies is Louisa's Professional Debut.

Louisa was also part of National Youth Theatre (2022), in the summer intake course. Louisa is now part of RADA's youth company, acting course.

Training credits: Saint Joan, The Winter's Tale and Dance Like Nobody Is Watching (Except Everyone Is).

Pearl Adams
Pearl trained at The BRIT School on the Theatre course. Flies is Pearl's Professional Debut.

Training credits: The Last Days of Judas Iscariot, As You Like It and Hedda Gabler and devised piece Cerebrum.

Afriya-Jasmine Nylander
Afriya-Jasmine trained at The BRIT School on the Theatre Course. This included The Bridge Company course. Flies is Afriya-Jasmine's Professional Debut.

Training credits: Three Sisters, An Invention, Troilus and Cressida and Are You Filming?

Ellie Rose Amit
Ellie-Rose trained at The BRIT School.

Other Credits: Pass It On theatre festival, The Camden Fringe Festival and Hana in the Amazon TV series, The Power.

Alongside acting, Ellie-Rose is also a writer.

Training credits: A Matter of Life and Death.

Willow Traynor

Rosa Amos

Annabel Gray

Louisa Hamdi

Pearl Adams

Afriya-Jasmine Nylander

Ellie Rose Amit

The Creative Team

Charlie Josephine | Writer
Charlie Josephine is an actor and a writer. They're passionate about making honest, visceral theatre. Particularly stories that centre working class women and queer people. Charlie's work includes Bitch Boxer (Soho Theatre), Massive (Audible) and I,Joan (The Globe). Charlie is this year's resident writer at Headlong Theatre and is also an associate artist at the NSDF. They're currently under commission at The RSC, Headlong Theatre and NT Connections.

Julia Head | Director
Julia is a director of live work from Bristol. She is the Artistic Director of FullRogue, a theatre company that exists to stress-test new writing and the limits of live performance. She is the Company Director of Young SixSix that collaborates closely with young people to make new work and supports them to realise their creative potential. Julia was a Headlong Origins Director for 2021 and is currently an Associate Artist at Bristol Old Vic, Associate Director of Twisted Theatre and a trustee of MAYK and Headlong. Recent Credits include: Romeo and Juliet (Bristol Old Vic), Massive (Audible Original Productions), Wild Swimming (BristolOldVic//59E59, NYC).

Cat Fuller | Designer
Cat Fuller has an MA in Performance Design from Bristol Old Vic Theatre School. In 2021 Cat was named a recipient of the Linbury Prize and was also awarded the John Elvery Prize for Excellence in Stage Design. Cat has an extensive specialist skill set, having previously worked as a Graphic Designer and Marketing Consultant within the arts. Cat has a particular interest in performance where theatre and music collide.

Her work as a set and costume designer includes The Sweet Science of Bruising (The Egg, Theatre Royal Bath), Romeo and Juliet (Bristol Old Vic), Kyoto (The Wardrobe Theatre), and The Duchess of Malfi (Putney Arts). Work as Set Designer includes The Three Seagulls (Bristol Old Vic) and Falling in Love Again (King's Head). Her work as an Associate Designer with Anna Fleischle includes: A Christmas Carol (Finnish National Opera and Ballet), Home I'm Darling (UK Tour), The Time Traveller's Wife (Chester Storyhouse) and Much Ado About Nothing (National Theatre) and for Katie Sykes: The Long Lie (Theatre Ad Infinitum).

Nandi Bhebhe | Movement Director

Nandi Bhebhe is a multi- disciplinary performer and maker, and trained at the Liverpool institute of Performing Arts. Nandi's credits include; Vocab Dance Companys Episodes of Blackness at Sadlers Wells, A Season in the Congo at The Young Vic, Bill T. Jones Fela! at the National Theatre and on Broadway, 'Wrath' for Channel 4s Random Acts, A Midsummer Nights Dream and Twefth Night at The Shakespeares Globe, Knee-high Theatres 946, The Tin Drum and UBU, A Monster Calls at The Old Vic, and most recently Wise Childrens Bagdad Cafe, Whistle Down the Wind and Othello at The Watermill Theatre, and Wuthering Heights at The National theatre and St Annes Warehouse, New York.

Nandi also co-direct works with artist Phoebe Davies as Bhebhe&Davies. Their work includes 'Creases', commissioned for the Tate Modern, and most recently 'Viscera', a short film for the Wellcome Collections On Happiness season.

Martha Godfrey | Lighting Designer

Martha Godfrey is a lighting and projection designer working across theatre, dance, musicals and live art. Past work includes: The Prince (Southwark Playhouse), Mapping Gender (Tour & The Place), Bangers (Tour & Soho Theatre), But I'm A Cheerleader (Turbine Theatre), Passion Fruit (New Diorama Theatre), Home, I'm Darling (Theatre Royal Bury St Edmunds), Oliver Twist! (Chester Storyhouse), What Do You See (Shoreditch Town Hall), Redemption (The Big House), Pink Lemonade (The Bush), Concrete Jungle Book (The Pleasance), Fever Pitch (The Hope), Around The World in Eighty Days (Theatre Royal Bury St Edmunds), Time and Tide (The Park), Before I Was A Bear (The Bunker), I Wanna Be Yours (UK Tour and Bush), Unknown Rivers (Hampstead Downstairs), We Dig (Ovalhouse), Cabildo (Arcola Theatre), GREY (Ovalhouse), WHITE (Ovalhouse, Pleasance Edinburgh Fringe, UK Tour), Exceptional Promise (The Bush), Fuck You Pay Me (The Bunker/Rich Mix/ Assembly Rooms, Edinburgh Fringe/Vaults Festival).

Nicole Raymond | Sound Designer

Nicole Raymond (NikNak) is an award winning storyteller who is developing her unique practice as a DJ & Turntablist, sound artist/ composer, music producer, events promoter, lecturer/tutor, sound engineer and radio presenter. Nicole is currently under commission with Sky and Opera North.

James Kent | AV Designer

James is a London-based director and film maker. He was Associate Director with the Bristol Old Vic Young Company and a resident artist at the Tobacco Factory Theatre. James has made work with Bristol Old Vic Theatre, Tobacco Factory Theatres, Young Vic, National Theatre, Headlong, The Lyric Hammersmith, Actors Touring Company, Company Three, Wardrobe Ensemble, Wardrobe Theatre, Fen and Insane Root.

Misha Mah | Production Manager
Misha is a freelance Production Manager currently based in London.
Credits include: Smoke (Southwark Playhouse), Zombiegate(Thea-
tre503), A Gig For Ghosts (Soho Theatre), The MP, Aunty Mandy, and
Me Curve Theatre), Far Gone (Roots Mbili, ZOO Southside), Caste-
ing (Paines Plough Roundabout), Hungry (Soho Theatre & Paines
Plough Roundabout), Kabul Goes Pop: Music Television Afghanistan
(Brixton House, Touring), Til Death Do Us Part (Theatre503). Misha
is currently Technical Manager at Theatre503.

Adriana Perucca | Company Stage Manager
Adriana trained at Rose Bruford College.
Selected credits include: Paradise Now! (Bush Theatre), Things I
Can Laugh About Now (Brixton House), The High Table (Bush Theatre),
Joan of Leeds (New Diorama), The Wolf of Wall Street Immersive
Experience (Site Specific, LDN), Confirmation (Pleasance, Edinburgh),
Strange Fruit (Bush Theatre), Hot Mess: Bezzie Mates (Soho
Theatre), Bottom (Soho Theatre), Counting Sheep (The Forge, Vaults)
and Dangerous Giant Animals (Theatre Row, NYC).

Katie Glassbrook | Assistant Stage Manager
Katie is currently on placement with Boundless, whilst training
at the Royal Academy of Dramatic Arts where she is specialising
in Stage Management and Wardrobe. Katie's most recent roles
include The Tempest (SM), Vincent in Brixton (DSM) and NSFW (ASM).
Alongside Katie's training, she has worked professionally at
'Wonderville' as ASM.

Elizabeth Anderson | Assistant Director
Elizabeth is currently on placement with Boundless, whilst
completing her degree at the University of Bristol where she is
studying English Literature and Film BA. Elizabeth's most recent
acting roles include Romeo and Juliet (Bristol Old Vic) and Macbeth
(Bearpit Theatre Company). Alongside this she has worked on
commercials with HunkyDoryFilms.

Flies rehearsal
photography by Ben North

Boundless Theatre

'And what a gift #ForBlackBoys is. You support and champion truly beautiful, necessary work that highlights often unseen voices'

- Shaniqua Benjamin, Croydon Poet Laureate

We support a community of young adults to be creative. Productions, projects and diverse experiences promote meaningful social engagement around culture. We're always in dialogue with a vibrant and diverse youth culture and believe by investing in and being inspired by early career artists we can promote conversation with a global community of 15-25-year-olds. Under the Artistic Direction of Rob Drummer since 2016, Boundless makes work across the UK and internationally, pioneering new ways to connect teenagers to theatre.

Our vision is for a world where all young adults harness their creativity to lead culture. Where intersectional and inclusive co-creation promotes radical optimism. Next generation ideas inspire the future of theatre as a vibrant, powerful tool for change and sociable space for community.

To find out more and get involved just say
hello@boundlesstheatre.org.uk

www.boundlesstheatre.org.uk
@boundlessabound
#weareboundless

Boundless Theatre is an Arts Council England National Portfolio Organisation

Registered charity no. 1089185

Boundless Team

Artistic Director & CEO	Rob Drummer
Executive Director	Ine Van Riet
Executice Director (mat cover)	Ellie Claughton
Head of Community	Daljinder Johal
Finance Manager	Mark Sands
Producer	Rowan Blake-Prescott
Talent Development Producer	Gabi Spiro
Social Media Manager	Gorga M'llaurie
Marketing & Audience Development Consultant	Zoe Biles
Boundless PR	Chloe Nelkin Consulting
Peggy Ramsay Foundation/ Film4 Awards Scheme Playwright	Natasha Brown
Boundless Accelerator 202	Jade Franks Yasmine Dankwah Chris Whyte On the Common

Boundless Advisory Group

The Boundless Advisory Group, made up of 15-25 year olds around the UK inform our strategy, voice their opinion on our work and share insight and guidance on our ambitious plans.

Email hello@boundlesstheatre.org.uk to find out more.

Finlay Ross Russell	Sadhana Narayanan
Cherry Eckel	Tolu Fagbayi
Aisling Lally	Liam Stone
Emilia Hargreaves	Xiggy Holding
Cliona Malin	Betty Williams-Singh
Julia Pilkington	

Boundless Board

Rosie Allimonos (Chair)	Alistair Wilkinson
Charlotte McMillan	Caspar Cech-Lucas
Spencer Simmons	Daze Aghaji FRSA
Natalie Chan	

*Phylisia Watkis (Company Secretary)

Boundless Drama Club

The Boundless Drama Club is for anyone starting out in theatre aged 15-25. Access funding, creative opportunities, workshops and advice in a diverse community.

Through online membership, you'll have access to high quality creative resources, challenges and masterclasses, mentoring and real time connections to peers and the Boundless team as well as our artists.

Since it's launch 2022, we've hosted writers groups and online and in-person workshops. We've built video, text and podcast content with experts, held artist networking, offered exclusive ticket deals and had 1:1s with some of our many Boundless Drama Club members.

Here's what our members are saying:

The best thing about Boundless Drama Club is "having a network of emerging theatre makers all in one place."

Our workshops are "friendly, engaging and supportive" and "knowledgable, kind and accessible".

But most of all, our members feel "really involved, valued and challenged in the best way."

If you're starting out in theatre, start with us.

www.boundlessdrama.club
#boundlessdramaclub

SHOREDITCH TOWN HALL

Welcoming thousands of people through its doors every year, Shoreditch Town Hall is a leading cultural, community and live events space housed in one of the grandest former civic buildings in the capital. Comprising over 48,000 square feet across seventy individual rooms, the Grade II-listed Town Hall is the largest multi-artform venue in Hackney and more widely used today than at any other point since being set up as a Charitable Trust in 1998.

The Town Hall presents a year-round cultural programme of progressive theatre, music, dance, circus and talks, as well as hosting numerous live-event hires ranging from documentary film premieres to tech conferences. The Town Hall supports artists by providing in-kind space for rehearsals and R&D residencies, and a permanent Artists Workspace where creatives can take advantage of a free desk space for administrative work. The organisation collaborates with a range of local partners to deliver an extensive community and engagement programme too.

Partnering with leading UK drama school Mountview, the Town Hall houses an MA in Site-Specific Theatre Practice and is also home to several local businesses, including the two Michelin-starred The Clove Club.

The Town Hall's programme has recently included work with The Cocoa Butter Club, Kakilang, LIFT, London International Mime Festival, Malborough Productions, New Earth Theatre, Nouveau Riche, Oliver Sim, The PappyShow; live talks with Craig David, Elizabeth Day, Louis Theroux, Mo Gawdat, Sophie Ellis-Bextor; events with the likes of Cartier, Costa Coffee, Jazz FM, Kerrang!, Kraken Rum, Shelter, Terrance Higgins Trust; and the filming of *The Death of Stalin*, *Florence Foster Jenkins*, *The Lady in the Van* and *Small Axe*.

Shoreditch Town Hall is a registered charity (1069617) and receives no regular or revenue funding, thus relying on 100% earned income every year.

SHOREDITCH TOWN HALL
380 Old Street, London, EC1V 9LT
020 7739 6176
www.shoreditchtownhall.com

@ShoreditchTH Twitter | Facebook | Instagram | TikTok | YouTube

SHOREDITCH
TOWN HALL
OLD STREET, LONDON, EC1

SHOREDITCH
TOWN HALL
OLD STREET, LONDON, EC1

CHARACTERS

GIRL ONE
GIRL TWO
GIRL THREE
GIRL FOUR
GIRL FIVE
GIRL SIX
GIRL SEVEN
JACK
PIGGY
RALPH
LITTLUN
MAN

AUTHOR'S NOTES

Cast

A group of genuinely diverse young women aged about fourteen. It's useful if the actors are a bit older, so they feel confident talking about puberty in hindsight. It'd be great if they can realistically play fourteen-year-olds though please. They'll need to be able to move, though not be trained dancers. They'll need to be able to confidently eyeball the audience. This piece is an invitation for them to feel empowered onstage, an experiment in a new free existence, a game against the male gaze.

Script Notes

Stage directions are in italics and brackets.

/ indicates a fast run onto the next line, almost an interruption.

/.. indicates where a word can't be found and something physical is expressed instead, a small gesture or a big abstract movement, whatever's honest.

Words that are crossed out like ~~this~~ are mouthed but not voiced.

PLEASURE ACTIVISM

Dr Zoë Svendsen re-energized me recently with her brilliant interrogation of what dramaturgy is. She provokes me to take responsibility for the political implications of my work. To be bold and dare to dream new futures. To work with a conscious awareness of the conversation my words are having with an actor, an audience, the theatre, the world. So I'm no longer interested in presenting problems in plays, without even the bare beginnings of an offer of some flawed solution. Because culture changes culture.

I am also inspired by the wonderful work of adrienne maree brown. I therefore want to offer the idea that pleasure (erotic and otherwise) is not only a survival mechanism in this hetero-ghetto, but a radical tool for activism, for social change, for revolution. It's surely impossible to feel pleasure whilst in a state of survival. And I want us to thrive. I'm fascinated by how we access, and harness, the power of pleasure within our movement towards freedom from patriarchy.

Therefore, here are some rules to support the pleasure activism that sits inside the dramaturgy of this play:

- Rigorous honesty and radical kindness between cast, creatives and crew is a non-negotiable must.
- Actively, and perhaps vocally, celebrating each other during rehearsals and /or performance is encouraged.
- Giggles fits, should they honestly arise during rehearsals and /or performance, are allowed. They are encouraged. They are to be indulged.
- Platonic physical intimacy between performers is encouraged. Clear, confident consent and detailed vocal feedback before during and after any physical touch is vital. Anything but a "full bodied yes" is a no.
- A courage and comfort box, filled with things that nourish and nurture, should be provided for the actors to have easy access to during rehearsals and /or performance. Therefore, an actor may collect or ask for fluffy slippers for example, or a handhold, or a cup of tea, to aid their work.
- Fun is necessary. This material is dark at times. Mental health comes first. Where possible play against the text. Explore cheekiness. Indulge in mischief.

THANK-YOUS

Huge thank you to Rob Drummer, all at Boundless Theatre and Shoreditch Town Hall for your tireless work on getting this production off the page and onto the stage. Thank you to the brilliant Bryony Shanahan, Jenni Jackson and Elayce Ismail for your work on the piece during R&Ds and workshops. Thank you to Erica Whyman, Ben Tyreman, Pippa Hill, Becky Latham and James Pidgeon for your support. Thank you, as always, to Jonathan at The Agency for your care. Huge thank you to Julia Head, who somehow creates the best rehearsal room, full of cheeky curiosity and deep belly laughter. Thank you to the beautiful cast, creative team and crew for this production of the play, you're all excellent and wonderful. Biggest thanks is to all the brilliant young people I met during the development of the script, your honesty and humour in the face of persistent male gaze violence was so inspiring.

(A vast empty stage. Downstage centre there is a small island of sand on the floor. One by one, a group of young women, at least thirty of them, walk from the wings to the sand-island. They each pause briefly before stepping onto it and turning to face us. The sand-island is barely big enough to fit everyone, so some jostling for space occurs, and perhaps some frustration spills out as passive-aggressive shoves or looks. Once they're settled they stand still, looking at us. It's quiet. They speak directly to us.)

GIRL ONE. You're looking at me.

(Silence.)

I can see you, looking at me.

(Silence.)

You're /

GIRL TWO. Looking at me.

GIRL THREE. I can see you /

GIRL THREE & FOUR. Looking at me /

GIRL FIVE. Looking /

GIRL SIX. Looking /

GIRL TWO & ONE. I can see you.

GIRL SEVEN. You're looking at me.

(They play a game with the audience. Repeating the phrase, "You're looking at me. I can see you, looking at me," over and

1

over in different ways. They gasp in faux surprise or genuine surprise, or pleasure, or coyness or pure joy at being looked at. They're clowning, being cheeky with us, it's fun. Suddenly, a CCTV camera, previously unnoticed, downstage right and pointing at the **GIRLS***, moves and makes a noise. They all freeze, rabbit in headlights. The atmosphere instantly changes. They hold their breath, trying not to want to look. The camera stops moving, pointing at them. Their eyes flash up to it, then back to us.)*

GIRL ONE. I can see you /

GIRL TWO. Looking at me.

GIRL THREE. And I can see you've got /

GIRL THREE & FOUR. No idea /

GIRL SEVEN. What it feels like to be seen.

GIRL FOUR. Can tell by that look in your eyes.

GIRL SIX & FIVE. Don't blink!

GIRL ONE. Or you'll miss it.

(Their eyes flash back up to the CCTV camera, then back to us, quicker than before. They readjust their clothes. The movement turns into a sort of squirm-dance over the next bit of text.)

GIRL FOUR. Yeah.

GIRL FIVE. Yeah you're looking at me.

GIRL FOUR. And I feel /

GIRL ONE. Shame.

GIRL SEVEN. Girls like me?

GIRL FIVE. We're full of it.

GIRL THREE. Because we're not enough /

GIRL TWO. We're just not enough /

GIRL FIVE. And you can see that /

GIRL SIX. And we can see that you can see that and there's nowhere to hide.

GIRL SEVEN. Want to rip our own skin off /

ALL GIRLS. *Crawling* /

GIRL ONE. Under your gaze, *this* shame?

GIRL THREE. It burns.

GIRL FOUR. And on the good days when we're half enjoying walking down the road in our body in the sunshine /

GIRL THREE. Sunshine /

GIRL ONE. Sunshine /

GIRL SIX. And a car pulls up /

GIRL FIVE. And he shouts out some shit /

GIRL ONE. Telling us we're fit /

GIRL SEVEN. *"Oi love"* /

GIRL FIVE. And yeah even if what he's saying is actually nice /

GIRL FOUR. It doesn't feel nice /

GIRL TWO. *"Oi love"* /

GIRL THREE. When he's all like /

GIRL TWO. *"Yeah baby yeah you look amazing!"*

GIRL SEVEN. It doesn't feel amazing it feels /

GIRL ONE. Violent.

      (Quiet.)

Because he can say that, with a confidence /

GIRL THREE. And a freedom /

GIRL TWO. Cus he's claiming the space /

GIRL SEVEN. See he's claiming the position of Looker. He's looking at us, we're being looked at.

GIRL ONE. Looking is privilege.

GIRL FOUR. The pleasure of viewing is a privilege that, ironically /

GIRL FOUR & THREE. He's blind to /

GIRL FIVE. Cus in the patriarchy /

GIRL FIVE & THREE. Men look /

GIRL FIVE. And women /

GIRL FIVE & SIX. Are looked at.

GIRL FOUR & TWO. Men do /

GIRL TWO. And women /

GIRL FOUR & TWO. Are done to /

GIRL SIX. So rape culture gets a whole new load of fuel.

GIRL ONE. And if you think we're being over the top you just watch how fast he gets ugly when we ask him to /

GIRL ONE & SEVEN. Stop.

GIRL FOUR. Our /

GIRL FOUR & THREE. 'No' /

GIRL FOUR. Threatens his masculinity /

GIRL FIVE. Caged animals are quick to /

GIRL FIVE & SEVEN. Bite /

GIRL SIX. And we're all caged by the patriarchy.

(They all shudder.)

ALL GIRLS. Ugh!

GIRL THREE. We don't even like that word.

GIRL FIVE. Who fucking, *'pat-ri-archy'*?!

> *(They shudder again, and the squirm-dance comes back over the next bit of text.)*

GIRL THREE. It sounds so /...

GIRL FOUR. Male.

GIRL TWO. We're learning that a lot of words do /

ALL GIRLS. *Sorry!*

GIRL SEVEN. That's probably our fault.

GIRL FIVE. We're learning how the P-word teaches us to blame ourselves.

ALL GIRLS. It's *our* fault /

GIRL SIX. If they're looking at us.

ALL GIRLS. It's *our* fault /

GIRL THREE. Cus we're *too much* /

GIRL TWO. Or *not enough.*

ALL GIRLS. It's *our* fault /

GIRL FOUR. If we're desired /

ALL GIRLS. It's *our* fault /

GIRL SIX. If we're raped /

ALL GIRLS. It's *our* fault /

GIRL ONE. If I'm fourteen.

> *(They all suddenly stop squirming, freeze in whatever position they're in.* **GIRL ONE** *speaks to the camera.)*

I'm fourteen years old. On the cusp of womanhood, and what I can see of what lies ahead I don't understand. I mean /

ALL GIRLS. *Is this it now?*

GIRL THREE. *Is this how it's going to be?*

GIRL FIVE. *Every day?*

GIRL FOUR. Sorry, but I just want to check that I've got this /

GIRL FOUR & TWO. Crystal clear /

GIRL FOUR. What you're asking of me.

(*The cheery and polite mask is slipping.*)

GIRL ONE. So from now on /

GIRL SIX. You're gonna watch me, yeah?

ALL GIRLS. *All the time?*

GIRL TWO. I hit puberty so now I'm prey?

GIRL THREE. And it's *my* job to be /

GIRL SEVEN. *Constantly* policing my own desirability because /

ALL GIRLS. (*To the camera.*) *Not enough* /

GIRL SEVEN. Gets me nothing and nowhere, but /

ALL GIRLS. (*To the camera.*) *Too much* /

GIRL SEVEN. And I'm asking for it?

GIRL FIVE. So either way /

ALL GIRLS. (*To the camera.*) *I'm* blamed /

GIRL THREE. For how /

ALL GIRLS. (*To the camera.*) *You* see me /

GIRL TWO. Is that right?

(*They move, neaten themselves up and calm themselves down. They smooth down hair, readjust clothes, wipe sweaty faces. They breathe, smile, and try again, 'cheery and polite'.)*

GIRL FIVE. I don't hate men.

GIRL FOUR. And I'm not gonna burn my bra.

GIRL THREE. I don't even really like the word feminist I just want to ask /

ALL GIRLS. *Is this it now?*

GIRL TWO. Because childhood was great. That was really fun.

(The 'cheery and polite' mask is slipping as the tempo picks up.)

GIRL SEVEN. But now my body is developing faster than my mind /

GIRL THREE. I'm not sure I've got the time to catch up with myself /

GIRL ONE. I can't help thinking who would I be if I wasn't thinking about being seen?

GIRL FOUR. Surely there's a better use of my time?

GIRL FIVE. But now a *huge* chunk of my brain space /

GIRL SIX. Is taken up with having to navigate *you* and your *looking*?

GIRL ONE. I mean how free would I be /

GIRL TWO. To think and /

GIRL THREE. Move and /

GIRL FOUR. Make shapes /

GIRL FIVE. And create?

GIRL SEVEN. I'd have so much more space inside my brain /

GIRL THREE. If I didn't have to spend so much /

GIRL THREE & TWO. Fucking time /

GIRL TWO. Thinking about if how I'm being seen is safe for me.

GIRL ONE. Because it's not a mere /

GIRL ONE & FOUR. Vanity /

GIRL ONE. Not a silly /

GIRL ONE & FOUR. Girly /

GIRL ONE. Complaint. But a desperate question of safety /

GIRL FOUR. Of survival /

ALL GIRLS. Am I safe?

GIRL SIX. Being seen like this /

GIRL THREE. Under your gaze /

GIRL FIVE. Your shame /

GIRL SEVEN. Infects every decision /

GIRL FOUR. Interrupts every thought /

GIRL SIX. *Constantly* checking myself /

GIRL THREE. *Constantly* on alert /

GIRL TWO. I don't feel safe /

GIRL TWO & SEVEN. I don't feel safe /

ALL GIRLS. I don't feel safe /

GIRL ONE. How can you expect me to be the best version of me when I'm scared like this?

(Quiet. They breathe.)

I'm tired, I'm /

GIRL SIX & SEVEN. So tired.

GIRL FOUR. We're only at the beginning, and already I'm /..

GIRL THREE. Because, for women, desire is shamed?

GIRL TWO. I am woman /

GIRL FIVE. And I desire /

GIRL THREE. And so I am shamed?

GIRL SIX. I am fourteen years old.

GIRL TWO. And already /

GIRL ONE. I'm fucking exhausted.

> *(Silence. Then a sudden burst into lights and noise. The **GIRLS** perform a movement sequence exploring puberty. It's fun and upbeat. **GIRL SIX** suddenly stops and speaks to us.)*

GIRL SIX. Game Three – Take Up Space.

> *(**GIRL SIX** joins back in with the dancing. **GIRL THREE** stops dancing, takes the centre, and begins a bit from* Lord of the Flies. *The others start to notice her and stop to watch. Someone signals to the tech box for the music to cut and it does.)*

GIRL THREE. *(As Piggy.)* She wants to know what you're going to do about The Beast? A Beastie. Ever so big. She saw it. A terrible Beastie, with claws and /

GIRL TWO. What are you doing?

GIRL THREE. Piggy, from *Lord of the Flies*. *(Looks at audience.)* I thought, aren't we doing *Lord of* /

GIRL FIVE. No! We're done with that. It's dead.

GIRL ONE. What?

GIRL TWO. It's boring!

GIRL ONE. Erm, it's a classic!

GIRL TWO. Who says?

GIRL THREE & ONE. Everyone!

GIRL FIVE. Nah it's shit. Honestly it's so boring.

GIRL SIX. Yeah we're not doing some dead white man story.

GIRL THREE. Isn't that like, what you're meant to do, in theatre? Shakespeare and that?

GIRL TWO. Another dead white bloke?

GIRL SEVEN. Yeah why're people *still* doing Shakespeare?

GIRL FOUR. Seriously!

GIRL ONE. I like Shakespeare.

GIRL FOUR. We're *not* doing Shakespeare!

GIRL FIVE. Dead, so dead!

GIRL ONE. Okay so what are we doing?

GIRL SIX. Anything we want! We could just /

> (**GIRL SIX** *looks around at the vast stage. She looks down at her feet, at the sand-island they're stuck on.* **GIRL SIX** *attempts to step off the sand-island. Everyone holds their breath. She changes her mind.*)

Here is good. We can do it from here.

GIRL THREE. Okay but, can I just be honest about something?

GIRL FOUR. Yeah?

GIRL THREE. Okay so like, when they said *come do some theatre, come make a play, about being young women* and all that. I was like, yeah yeah yeah cool, but then actually /.. Okay, this might sound a bit dumb, but I was like, oh *fuck I actually don't know what I wanna say!* Like, we have to fight so much to just even get the chance to "take up space" and then when you finally get it, it's like oh shit! /.. Like I actually dunno what I wanna say because I've just been so focused on /

GIRL SEVEN. Getting the chance to?

GIRL THREE. Yeah!

GIRL SEVEN. Yeah.

GIRL THREE. So I just thought maybe it'd be cool, to do, like, something we wouldn't normally get to? Like a classic, like *Lord of the Flies* or whatever. But to do it *our* way. Put a modern twist on it.

GIRL TWO. That is kinda cool.

GIRL FOUR. Yeah it is but like you could do *anything*! Why do some dead white bloke?

GIRL SEVEN. Yeah like no offence but, is it *really* that interesting to do a 'modern take on a classic'?

GIRL FOUR. Exactly. I wanna hear what *you've* gotta say!

GIRL ONE. Yeah but that's like so much pressure on us?!

GIRL THREE. Yeah!

GIRL SEVEN. Okay okay, so what if we took a story, like a classic one, as like a framework? As like /

GIRL TWO. A road map?

GIRL SEVEN. Yeah. To help us, like, navigate /

GIRL FOUR. Misogyny.

GIRL FIVE. Rah! Deep!

GIRL FOUR. Okay, but they are actually all dead white men. The writers. And all the main parts are boys. Look, Peter Pan and the Lost *Boys*. Of Mice and *Men*.

GIRL FIVE. That's racist.

GIRL SIX. Yeah fuck that.

GIRL FOUR. Oliver Twist. James Bond. Harry Potter.

GIRL FIVE. Nah nah nah!

GIRL THREE. Terf!

GIRL TWO. Haha yeah seriously we can't endorse that.

GIRL ONE. Okay okay. Nothing by she-who-shall-not-be-named.

GIRL SIX. Okay erm. *The Jungle Book*?

GIRL SEVEN. 1984.

GIRL SIX. *Robinson Crusoe*.

GIRL SEVEN. *Huckleberry Finn*.

GIRL SIX. *The Catcher in the Rye*.

GIRL SEVEN. *One Flew Over the Cuckoo's Nest*.

GIRL FIVE. Ok, I think we get the /

GIRL FOUR. *Dracula*!

GIRL ONE. *A Christmas Carol*?

GIRL TWO. *A Clockwork Orange*.

GIRL SEVEN. A Curious Tale of The Dog of the, tale of the, whatever.

GIRL THREE. *The Odyssey*.

GIRL FOUR. *Waiting for Godot*.

GIRL ONE. *Wind in the Willows*.

GIRL FIVE. I like that one!

GIRL SEVEN. *Treasure Island*.

GIRL SIX. *Sweeney Todd*.

GIRL SEVEN. *Threepenny Opera. Uncle Vanya. Edward the Third. Richard the Third. The Great Gatsby. The Hobbit. King Arthur. King Lear. King John. James and the Giant Peach. The Merchant of Venice. Julius Caesar. Coriolanus. Titus Andronicus. Othello.* Henry the Fourth, Fifth, Sixth, Twenty-Seventh. Part one part two part three. *Animal Farm. Lord of the Rings.*

*(**GIRL SEVEN** can improvise more names of stories written by men about men.)*

Lord of the Flies.

(They all roll their eyes. Then suddenly play characters, with big, booming posh-boy voices.)

JACK. Halt! We heard a horn being blown, where's the man?

RALPH. There is no man! Only me!

JACK. Isn't there a ship then? Isn't there a man here?

PIGGY. We're having a meeting. So we can decide what to do. We've got to take names, and then we can /

JACK. You're talking too much! Shut up, Fatty!

(They all laugh shrilly.)

RALPH. He's not Fatty, his real name's Piggy!

JACK. Piggy?!

*(They all burst into loud laughter. **PIGGY** is suddenly very interested in cleaning their glasses. **RALPH** takes the conch.)*

How are we going to be rescued?

RALPH. Seems we ought to have a chief to decide things.

ALL GIRLS. A chief! A chief!

JACK. I ought to be chief! Because I'm chapter chorister, I can sing C-sharp and /

GIRL FOUR. Nah I'm not into that. Let's do something else!

GIRL THREE. No it's good, honestly, let's fast-forward a bit.

*(The **GIRL**'s fast-forward. **PIGGY** steps up.)*

PIGGY. She wants to know what you're going to do about The Beast? A Beastie. Ever so big. She saw it. A terrible

Beast, that came in the dark and wanted to *eat her*! She says she saw it, she says *it will come back tonight*!

GIRL FIVE. Nah that's rubbish! 'Bout a load of stupid posh boys?

GIRL SEVEN. Exactly! All of these stories. Are told by men /

GIRL TWO. About men /

GIRL SEVEN. For men.

(*Beat.*)

GIRL FIVE. Where's the bits for us?

GIRL SIX. Exactly.

GIRL FIVE. Nah. They can't do that!

GIRL SIX. Exactly /

GIRL SEVEN. They *have* done that! We've been totally excluded.

GIRL FIVE. Cunts!

GIRL SIX. Exactly!

GIRL FIVE. Nah but... *I* want a sword fight!

GIRL THREE. I want good lines. I want great big speeches.

GIRL ONE. Yeah! And I want a pirate ship, yeah, massive sea battle /

GIRL FOUR. Yeah I wanna win the war, and win the girl and /

GIRL TWO. Maybe not the *girl*.

GIRL FOUR. Yeah the girl.

GIRL TWO. Okay, well, yeah whatever floats your /

GIRL THREE. Win whoever you fancy!

GIRL SIX. Maybe not *win*. We don't *win* people. They're not /

GIRL SEVEN. Prizes. They're not /

GIRL SIX. Objects.

GIRL FOUR. In stories they are.

GIRL TWO. Anyway. Take your pick, it's basically the fucking same all over, so.

GIRL SIX. All the stories /

GIRL SEVEN. The entire cannon /

GIRL TWO. Hah! Cannon!

GIRL FIVE. Hang on. *All* of them?

GIRL ONE. Yeah.

GIRL FIVE. Woah.

GIRL ONE. Yeah.

> *(Beat. They all feel the weight of the patriarchy.)*

GIRL FIVE. Feels so /..

GIRL FOUR. Yeah.

> *(Beat.)*

GIRL THREE. I tried to talk to my dad about this and he /

GIRL TWO. Didn't listen?

> *(She shakes her head. Quiet.)*

GIRL ONE. What if we chopped out their tongues? Then they couldn't /

GIRL TWO. Interrupt us, anymore?

GIRL FOUR. *(To us.)* Game Six – Off With Their Tongues!

> *(Music. A shift in space. They pulse to the beat, building in confidence and power.)*

GIRL SEVEN. We could call a National Medical Screening. Pass some, Legislation, make it /

GIRL THREE. A Legal Requirement /

GIRL FOUR. That every man *immediately* goes to his local doctor's surgery.

GIRL TWO. Threaten them with Cancer /

GIRL FIVE. Or entice them with Penis Enlargement /

GIRL SIX. Or give then no explanation at all /

GIRL FOUR. Just *insist* they get down there /

GIRL THREE. *Immediately!*

GIRL FIVE. Or face some awful Punishment.

GIRL SIX. We'll give them a day off work to recover /

GIRL THREE. Because we're nice like that /

GIRL FOUR. And that's what nice people would do.

GIRL ONE. So they'd all leave their jobs /

GIRL FIVE. The *entire country* would be at a standstill /

GIRL THREE. Every, single, man /

GIRL FOUR. Thousands and thousands /

GIRL TWO. Up and down the country /

GIRL SEVEN. Queuing at the quacks!

GIRL SIX. The press would have a field day /

GIRL THREE. Until it's *their* time to cue up too.

GIRL ONE. And one by one they'd see the doctor. Say ah.

ALL GIRLS. *Ahhhh!*

GIRL ONE. Snip!

GIRL FIVE. Pluck them out /

GIRL THREE. Sew them up /

GIRL FOUR. Give them a lolly /

GIRL SEVEN. And send 'em on their way.

GIRL TWO. By teatime they'd all be silent /

GIRL ONE. Mute!

>   *(Quiet.)*

>   Perhaps you think I'm being too, aggressive. You think I'm trying to shock for the sake of being shocking? Think I'm being silly, being, grotesque, being a bit O-T-T?

GIRL TWO. But then you think about rape.

GIRL SIX. Centuries, of rape /

GIRL FOUR. And abuse /

GIRL SEVEN. And FGM /

GIRL THREE. And murder.

GIRL ONE. And all of the little everyday things /

GIRL FOUR. The little everyday comments /

GIRL SIX. Little everyday looks /

GIRL THREE. Little everyday turns of phrases /

GIRL ONE. Every *single* word every *single* interruption every *single* silencing and you add *all of them up* and question if *I'm* being violent? Question if I'm being aggressive, being a bit O-T-T?! I think you'll see that actually /

GIRL TWO. Actually /

GIRL THREE. Actually /

GIRL FOUR. I think /

GIRL SIX. You'll see that /

GIRL ONE. I'm not even touching the sides.

(Quiet.)

GIRL SIX. And, *yes*.

GIRL THREE. Of course.

GIRL TWO. In, *reality*.

GIRL THREE. It doesn't solve much /

GIRL FIVE. Doesn't solve much /

GIRL FOUR. Doesn't solve much at *all*.

GIRL ONE. Maybe cutting out their fucking tongues doesn't solve a single fucking thing. But /

GIRL SEVEN. It might make us feel better.

GIRL FOUR. And I think /

GIRL THREE. I think /

GIRL FIVE. Actually /

GIRL ONE. I think that's valid. I do.

(Quiet.)

GIRL TWO. The writer would like to take this opportunity, to make it really clear, that she doesn't hate men.

GIRL ONE. No, not at all.

GIRL TWO. She actually really likes them.

GIRL SEVEN. Bits of them more than others.

GIRL FIVE. Jheeze!

GIRL THREE. No, but seriously /

GIRL FOUR. Let's get serious /

GIRL FIVE. For real for real!

GIRL SEVEN. This isn't 'man hating.'

GIRL FIVE. Nah!

GIRL TWO. It is, you know, feminist, but it's really not /

GIRL FIVE. Hating on like, *all* men /

GIRL FOUR. That's not what feminism means!

GIRL FIVE. Obviously.

GIRL FOUR. "Obviously"?

GIRL ONE. We don't hate men /

GIRL TWO. We *don't* hate men /

GIRL FIVE. Nah.

GIRL THREE. Men are not the problem /

GIRL FIVE. Nah.

GIRL SIX. But the problem is men /

GIRL FIVE. Eh?

GIRL SEVEN. The problem is male.

GIRL FIVE. Ah okay, yeah, yeah I get you.

GIRL SIX. Yeah?

GIRL FIVE. Yeah. It's just /..

GIRL FOUR. What?

GIRL FIVE. Don't you think this is all getting a bit /.. Like, why's the writer talking, through us. Isn't that weird?

GIRL SEVEN. Isn't that what all writers do?

GIRL FIVE. I dunno it just seems a bit /..

GIRL THREE. Intense?

GIRL FIVE. Yeah. A bit fierce.

GIRL FOUR. She does seems a bit, angry.

(They all grimace and nod.)

GIRL ONE. I bet she's single.

GIRL THREE. I bet she's a lesbian.

GIRL TWO. I bet she's a feminist.

> *(They all roll their eyes in unison and laugh. The camera suddenly zooms and they all freeze, instantly terrified. Once it's settled, and they've exhaled, they are angry. They clench their jaws and their firsts, wishing they could rip that fucking camera down. **PIGGY** suddenly reappears, perhaps with a plastic pig nose pulled on.)*

PIGGY. Well I think. Actually yes, I really do, I think we need to use the conch again.

> *(The **GIRLS** creep in around her, menacing, grateful for somewhere to channel this ugly energy. **PIGGY** tries her best to stay calm.)*

When, when we want to speak. Because... because it's, it's the rules. You've got to have rules, you've got /

ALL GIRLS. Kill the pig, spill its blood, kill the pig /

PIGGY. That's not funny! Jack? Jack? That's not funny! That's not /

ALL GIRLS. Kill the pig! Spill its blood! Kill the pig! Spill its blood! Kill the pig! Spill its blood!

> *(They crowd around **PIGGY** menacingly. Just as they look like they're about to swallow her whole, one **GIRL** suddenly turns out to us, a dark stain at the front of her shorts. A **LITTLUN** points at the **GIRL**'s legs, staring open-mouthed in horror. The **GIRL** watches blood trickle down the inside of her own thigh. She looks terrified. Everyone stares.)*

LITTLUN. The Beast!

JACK. No.

LITTLUN. The Beast got her /

RALPH. There *is* no beast!

LITTLUN. Then what's *that*?!

(Silence.)

Are you, dying?

JACK. No, she's a woman.

(They do a "it-feels-good-to-be-a-woman" dance, and we enjoy the surprising burst of genuine joy. Light and noise and energy. A school bell rings.)

GIRL FOUR. So suddenly, I'm fourteen /

GIRL THREE. I'm fourteen and /

GIRL ONE. Oh my god /

GIRL SIX. Oh my god /

GIRL SEVEN. Oh my god /

GIRL TWO. I'm a woman. Like, overnight.

ALL GIRLS. *Fuck!*

GIRL SIX. I got boobs really early and like, they did not fuck around.

GIRL THREE. Some girls are really shy about it /

GIRL FIVE. Yeah, I'm not really that bothered.

GIRL SEVEN. Seeing that all of my other friends are nowhere near that?

GIRL ONE. The classic – getting my period for the first time /

GIRL FOUR. Oh my god /

GIRL ONE. Really freaked me out.

GIRL TWO. There's suddenly hair on my vagina?!

GIRL FIVE. *Fuck!*

GIRL ONE. Like, I really freaked out /

GIRL TWO. Like, what the actual fuck?

GIRL SIX. Suddenly you've got boobs you don't know what to do with /

GIRL THREE. It's a *fuck load* of hair!

GIRL TWO. Just like, *there* all of a sudden /

GIRL THREE. All of a sudden /

GIRL TWO. Like, *boom*, bush?!

GIRL SEVEN. I started shaking /

GIRL FIVE. *Fuck!*

GIRL ONE. Went running to my mum /

GIRL THREE. I didn't get armpit hair for ages.

GIRL SIX. I mean they're not *massive* /

GIRL SEVEN. They're bigger than most of my friends'.

GIRL THREE. Everyone else has got it, why haven't I?

GIRL TWO. Oh my god you're so lucky /

GIRL SEVEN. Don't you shave your legs?

GIRL ONE. I had all the necessary education /

GIRL FOUR. About what it is and what to expect /

GIRL ONE. But when it was actually was there /

GIRL TWO. In my knickers?

GIRL FIVE. *Fuck!*

GIRL SEVEN. Aren't bodies amazing?!

GIRL SIX. Yeah!

GIRL SEVEN. Like, anatomically, it's really quite an amazing /

GIRL SIX. Transformation /

GIRL SEVEN. Yeah! From this sweaty kid, to a /

GIRL SIX. Beautiful butterfly!

GIRL SEVEN. Ah! Thanks babes!

GIRL ONE. I was freaking out!

GIRL THREE. Aren't you wearing bras yet?

GIRL FOUR. So happy I'm finally not an A-cup anymore!

GIRL FIVE. Have you started your period yet?

GIRL FOUR. Cus everyone loves big boobies don't they?

GIRL ONE. Suddenly you can smell the deep dark secret inside smells of the girl next to you.

GIRL THREE. And now it grows there I'm like, oh fucking hell /

GIRL SIX. Why's it brown?!

GIRL TWO. It's so long?!

GIRL ONE. And you know this means she can smell yours too.

GIRL SEVEN. Do you fancy him?

GIRL FOUR. It's just weird at first cus it's like, bam bam bam /

GIRL FIVE. Change after change /

GIRL ONE. And suddenly you really *really* want to smell your own.

GIRL THREE. Your body is different /

GIRL SIX. Everyone's looking at you different /

GIRL TWO. Change after change /

GIRL ONE. Smell to check, to know.

GIRL SEVEN. Are you still a virgin?

GIRL FOUR. I was freaked out /

GIRL TWO. Like, woah!

GIRL ONE. Slow down!

GIRL THREE. Thinking like, *fuck* /

GIRL SIX. This is a big deal /

GIRL ONE. Like I'm not a little girl anymore /

GIRL SEVEN. I'm a woman now!

GIRL FIVE. *Fuck!*

GIRL THREE. I wasn't embarrassed by it /

GIRL TWO. No /

GIRL FOUR. Course not /

GIRL SIX. I'm not embarrassed /

GIRL THREE. It just makes you question like /

GIRL FIVE. Oh my god /

GIRL ONE. Oh my god /

GIRL TWO. Oh my god /

GIRL SEVEN. Am I normal?

GIRL FOUR. Oh my god, am I normal?

> *(They suddenly lift their T-shirts up over their faces. Projected onto their bare bellies are video clips of girl bands, Photoshopped models, pornography, lions chasing zebras, ultra-scans of the brain, overly sexualized images of women in adverts for cars and beers and protein powder. The* **GIRLS** *lower their T-shirts and stare wide-eyed at us, some of them still have a hand over their mouth, some have an index finger in their mouth like*

a fishhook. The video ends, and they slowly lower their T-shirts. They re-adjust their clothes, suddenly embarrassed, smooth down their hair, neaten themselves up. Breathe. Force a smile.)

GIRL TWO. *(To us.)* Game Eight – How Not To Get Raped.

GIRL SEVEN. I'm thirteen and some bloke stopped his car by me, and he was like *oh do I know you from somewhere blah blah blah*, and I was like *no, you don't*.

GIRL SIX. Don't wear that, it's not worth it.

GIRL FIVE. No, don't get a taxi! Are you mad?

GIRL SIX. Don't walk home alone!

GIRL FIVE. Not after dark!

GIRL SIX. Okay but stay on the phone to me yeah?

GIRL FIVE. Keys between your fingers.

GIRL SIX. Ready to run.

GIRL FIVE. Ready to run.

GIRL SIX. Text me when you're home.

GIRL FIVE. Love you /

GIRL SIX. Love you /

GIRL FIVE. Love you /

GIRL SEVEN. And I kept walking and he was following me in his car, all like, *come on don't be like that* and I was like /.. Okay so even if, like I don't actually know *how* your intention could be *nice*, as in, I can't think how, cus it's *just scary*, I'm *just scared*, like what the fuck do you do?

GIRL THREE. Yeah. That's yeah. Like one hundred. I remember the first time I was eleven /

GIRL TWO. Because I looked. I started getting different body shape really early /

GIRL THREE. So my face looked eleven but my body didn't.

GIRL TWO. I can't remember all of what he said /

GIRL ONE. But I definitely knew at the time /

GIRL TWO. It wasn't something you should be saying /

GIRL SIX. To an eleven-year-old girl.

GIRL SEVEN. I was walking home from school with my friend and this car slows down, and we know already something is gonna happen. And this man, points at us and does this. *(She does the wanking sign.)* He even did a face. Like a jizz face.

GIRL FIVE. Haha that's funny!

GIRL SIX. It's not.

GIRL SEVEN. He did it *knowing* we couldn't do anything back. Like his intention, was to hurt us, he did it deliberately to make us feel shit. Then drove off.

GIRL FOUR. Oh god yeah! They're the *worst*!

GIRL TWO. Yeah!

GIRL FOUR. Then you're just left there feeling totally *shit*!

GIRL TWO. Yeah!

GIRL SIX. Drive-by shame bombs!

(They all shudder.)

GIRL SEVEN. I got way more of it when I was in school uniform. Which is like so fucked up! Cus that's like visual proof that I'm underage!

GIRL SIX. The schoolgirl fetish.

GIRL FIVE. Porn!

GIRL SEVEN. I don't wanna be porn!

GIRL THREE. Yeah! And like, that was the first time I realized /

GIRL FIVE. Like woah /

GIRL TWO. Men see my body /

GIRL SIX. And think of things /

GIRL FOUR. That I don't want them to be thinking about.

GIRL THREE. And it's just scary because /

GIRL ONE. There's not really anything you can do about it.

GIRL FIVE. Like, seriously /

GIRL TWO. What can I do?!

GIRL SIX. Wear a jacket?

GIRL SEVEN. Don't go out alone /

GIRL TWO. Ring me when you're home /

GIRL SIX. Keys between your fingers /

GIRL SEVEN, TWO & THREE. Stay safe!

GIRL FIVE. That's what they say isn't it?

GIRL ONE. Teaching us how not to get raped.

GIRL SIX. Yeah! Like, I dunno who started that? I dunno the history of it, like the mythology of rape or whatever. Like, I've not exactly *studied* it, so I dunno but like, it seems at *some* point in history, *someone* decided it'd be a good idea to teach women how not to get sexually assaulted. Rather than teaching men to not attack women. Like yeah, let's spend *all* of our time and resources and energy or whatever, teaching women how *not* to get attacked. How to avoid it. As though men are wild animals that we need to take care around? Don't poke the bear in the zoo, it's only *natural* that wild animals will be wild, it's only *natural* that men will want to attack women so be careful girls! So then like, it's your fault, if you are attacked. Cus obviously you must have not followed the excellent guidance we provided. Obviously you're stupid and you're not keeping yourself safe, and actually you probably wanted it. So not only are you attacked, but then you're shamed for it? And then the laws, that are written by men, makes it pretty much impossible for you to successfully convict a rapist. I mean, wow! What a fucking brilliant way of oppressing women. That is, an *incredible* tool of the patriarchy. It's actually, really impressive.

GIRL FOUR. I can't really remember the last time I didn't go out and someone like winked at me /

GIRL TWO. Or shouted at me /

GIRL THREE. Or whistled at me /

GIRL SEVEN. Or asked for my number.

GIRL FOUR. And the second, they always get *so shocked* when I'm like *I'm fourteen!*

GIRL ONE. *I'm fifteen!*

GIRL FIVE. *I'm twelve!*

GIRL THREE. And they're like *oh my god I'm so sorry I'm so sorry!*

GIRL SEVEN. And it's like, they're sorry when I'm fourteen /

GIRL FOUR. But the fact that they'd approach any woman like that?

GIRL TWO. The first time it happened I was so shocked /

GIRL SEVEN. *Oh my god, what the fuck?!*

GIRL ONE. It's not until later that I *realised*, like, actually that is a problem.

GIRL FOUR. It's not something women should just accept.

GIRL THREE. Like it is an *actual* problem.

GIRL TWO. But because it's so common /

GIRL SEVEN. You see it happening to your aunties /

GIRL FOUR. You see it happening to your mum's friends /

GIRL TWO. D'you know what I mean? You see it /

GIRL FIVE. See it happen to all the women around you /

GIRL SEVEN. From a really young age.

GIRL THREE. So when it starts happening to you you're like /

GIRL FOUR. Okay /

GIRL SEVEN. It's just a normal part of /

GIRL THREE. Like it *is* normal, but it shouldn't be.

GIRL SIX. If I'm on my own /

GIRL FOUR. I mean I have to judge the situation.

GIRL ONE. If I'm on my own then I just keep walking /

GIRL SIX. Just keep walking /

GIRL TWO. Keep walking /

GIRL FIVE. Keep my head down /

GIRL SEVEN. Head down /

GIRL ONE. Head down, keep walking /

GIRL TWO. Keep walking.

> *(They do the 'keep-walking dance.' Pressure builds up until they exhale, refuge is found in the cinema.)*

GIRL FOUR. My dad took us to see the new *Blade Runner*. I'm not really into that but, my little brother wanted to go and, we only see my dad at weekends and, whatever. I love going to the cinema, share a big box of popcorn, sweet *and* salty, obvs. Massive thing of Sprite with ice. The film starts and, I've not even seen the first one so

I've got no idea what's going on. And it's all sci-fi and gun fights and blowing shit up. My brother is *loving it* he's so excited! Me and my dad keep looking across at him and laughing, his face is so like, *wow* this is *amazing*! Because yeah, who wouldn't want to be Ryan Gosling with a gun, and a cool coat or, Harrison what's his name. Sure, shooting each other and saying cool stuff, great. But. All the women in that film are like, naked, like totally naked for *no reason* what so ever?! One of them is literally a robot sex slave who like superimposes herself onto a prostitute so he can fuck her? I was *so embarrassed*! Sat there with my *dad*?! Proper blushing like, *oh my god get me out of here!* My little brother leans across and whispers to me, *why is she naked?* And I was like, *I don't know.* I don't know.

GIRL SEVEN. The writer would like to take this opportunity to assure you that she's well aware you can totally /

GIRL SIX. They.

GIRL SEVEN. What?

GIRL SIX. They, not she.

GIRL SEVEN. Oh!

GIRL SIX. Yeah.

GIRL SEVEN. Oh okay, *they*, cool.

GIRL TWO. I *knew* they'd be queer! You can just tell.

GIRL FIVE. Yeah!

GIRL SEVEN. Anyway. The writer, would like to take this opportunity to assure you that they are well aware you can totally /

ALL GIRLS. "Hears the writer's voice!"

GIRL SEVEN. They know! And they're not bothered.

GIRL ONE. In fact, they're pleased you can hear it /

GIRL FIVE. Loud and fucking clear.

GIRL SEVEN. Because actually, perhaps that's a rule set up for *male* writers /

GIRL TWO. To help them avoid waffling on /

GIRL ONE. Or preaching /

GIRL SIX. Or mansplaining.

GIRL SEVEN. And perhaps, in this piece /

GIRL FIVE. Written by, someone assigned female at birth /

GIRL FOUR. About the female experience /

GIRL ONE. Of being objectified /

GIRL TWO. And silenced /

GIRL FIVE. And ignored.

GIRL THREE. It makes more sense /

GIRL SEVEN. That their voice is explicitly /

GIRL FOUR. And unapologetically /

GIRL SIX. Present. And yes /

GIRL FIVE. We're preaching.

GIRL SEVEN. Are we?

GIRL SIX. And yes /

GIRL FIVE. We're angry.

GIRL THREE. And that's okay /

GIRL FIVE. That's okaaaaaaaaay!

GIRL FOUR. Of course we're angry

GIRL TWO. We're really fucking angry.

GIRL SEVEN. Who wouldn't be?

GIRL FIVE. Yeah but like. I dunno. I just wanna be! I just wanna exist! I don't want to have to keep being this

like, strong independent woman. I don't wanna /..
Why've I always gotta be loud, and revolutionary and,
an activist, all the time? What if I just wanna be quiet?

GIRL ONE. I hear that.

GIRL THREE. Yeah me too.

GIRL SEVEN. It is interesting that the writer has popped
up here, in the script, like they're nervous of how
they're being perceived, so they're doing this cheeky
commentary on their own work. It's like a sneaky
apology for their politics in case they're being read as,
too much, too what, aggressive?

GIRL FIVE. Yeah but would you say that if they were a man
though?

GIRL SEVEN. How'd you mean?

GIRL FIVE. Like people blatantly wouldn't! You'd call it
like, powerful or /

GIRL THREE. Punchy?

GIRL FIVE. Yeah, or bold.

GIRL THREE. Yeah but if it was softer, and written by a
man it'd be described as like,

GIRL FIVE. Delicate /

GIRL THREE. Intricate /

GIRL FIVE. Nuanced.

GIRL THREE. Haha yeah. But the same piece written by a
woman?

GIRL FIVE. Whimsical, flowery /

GIRL THREE. Self indulgent.

GIRL FIVE. Ugh yeah of course.

GIRL SEVEN. So are you saying our reactions to work are
gendered?

GIRL FIVE & THREE. Yeah!

GIRL SEVEN. Hmm, that's interesting.

> *(They all ponder. Suddenly a song in the style of Beyoncés* **[END OF TIME]** *bursts on, and we launch into a full-on dance routine. Despite the tiny sand-island that they are squeezed onto, the* **GIRLS** *do Queen B proud. It is fierce and fabulous and fun. An absolute celebration of all things woman. Then we see them dancing like no one is looking, alone in their rooms. Then see them dancing together like they're in a club. Suddenly in the middle of all this joy, the camera zooms in on them making the lights and sound warp, and the* **GIRLS***' movement slow. Their faces drop to deadpan as they feel the camera looking at them.* **GIRL FOUR** *suddenly starts drowning. It's horrible. Choking and spluttering and gasping for air. The* **OTHER GIRLS** *ignore it, deadpan. Then, suddenly, everything jumps back up to full speed and lights and sound. The* **GIRLS** *finish the dance, but the camera has tainted it, and their faces are deadpan, numb.)*

GIRL ONE. *(To us.)* Game Nine – Body Count.

GIRL TWO. Yeah, they're all watching porn.

ALL GIRLS. *Ping!*

GIRL FIVE. Everyone's is /

GIRL TWO. It's everywhere /

GIRL SIX. *Ping!*

GIRL FOUR. I don't think parents and teachers and stuff realise, but like /

GIRL FIVE. *Ping!*

GIRL SEVEN. He's always watched a lot of porn.

GIRL TWO. I can tell within about two seconds. Honestly it's ruining my sex life.

GIRL THREE. By the time I was like twelve I'd seen *everything* /

GIRL FOUR. *Ping!*

GIRL TWO. They copy what they see on there /

GIRL SEVEN. Sometimes we watch it together /

GIRL TWO. And, honestly, it makes me *fucking hate* the women for pretending /

GIRL ONE. And now the boys look at you differently /

GIRL TWO. Cus then I have to pretend /

GIRL ONE. Look at your body /

GIRL TWO. And oh, it don't half go on!

GIRL THREE. It makes you look at yourself differently yeah /

GIRL FOUR. Makes you question like /

GIRL SEVEN. *Ping!*

GIRL FIVE. Am I meant to look like that?

GIRL TWO. Quick lick and they shove a finger up there, really hard, and think that's foreplay?!

GIRL SEVEN. He can be a bit rough sometimes. *(Shrugs.)*

GIRL THREE. *Ping!*

GIRL FIVE. Should I make noises like that?

GIRL SIX. They shove it in so hard, bang bang bang bang bang /

GIRL TWO. They always want to jizz on your face /

GIRL FIVE. Should I pull faces like that?

GIRL SIX. Hammering away for hours like they're digging some hole in the ground?

GIRL ONE. I remember hating sex before I even had it /

GIRL SIX. I'm like, helloooooooooo!

GIRL TWO. Being a virgin was this horrible secret.

GIRL FOUR. *Ping!*

GIRL TWO. I just wanted to do it so it was done.

GIRL ONE. *Ping!*

GIRL THREE. Barbie fannies. That's what my mum calls it. She's so embarrassing!

GIRL SEVEN. He sends me them to watch.

GIRL THREE. She says it's porn making us all do it but I don't think it is.

GIRL SEVEN. And he's like, *oi babes, let's do this yeah?*

GIRL THREE. It's just fashion, plus it's more hygienic isn't it /

GIRL SEVEN. And at first, if I'm honest, it made me feel a bit sick /

GIRL THREE. Urgh, yeah, having hair there is so disgusting, it's gross /

GIRL SEVEN. But I watched it anyway /

GIRL THREE. It's not natural, you've got to be smooth. From the eyelashes down.

GIRL ONE. You can get surgery now. To fix your lips. Down there. To make them like, more tidy.

GIRL THREE. Oh my god no!

GIRL SIX. Bang bang bang bang bang!

GIRL FOUR. Boys will just straight up ask you, *how many people have you slept with?*

GIRL TWO. It's fucking 'em up, honestly, it's really bad.

GIRL FOUR. 'Body count.' Urgh, I hate that.

GIRL SIX. *Ping!*

GIRL SEVEN. The boys in school are worse.

GIRL ONE. Oh god yeah!

GIRL SEVEN. They sexually harass *all* the time! And teachers are like *oh well you know* /

GIRL SIX. *Boys will be boys!*

GIRL THREE. But it's horrible! It's actually really horrible!

GIRL FOUR. Yeah! It's like *mate, I'm tryna do my maths!*

GIRL FIVE. Haha yeah! Like *I'm in geography, no I dont wanna suck your dick!*

GIRL SIX. They're saying shit *all* the time!

GIRL THREE. It's constant!

GIRL SIX. Someone needs to teach the boys better /

GIRL SEVEN. Before they grow into men.

GIRL FIVE. Innit!

GIRL FOUR. I stopped doing sport.

GIRL FIVE. Oh no!

GIRL FOUR. Yeah I just. Couldn't take it anymore. All the comments and, them laughing at me and /.. Cus my boobs move when I run? Like, big deal? And I get sweaty, so what? It's normal to get sweaty when you run!

GIRL ONE. Most girls don't feel comfortable talking about it. Masturbation?

ALL GIRLS. Oh my God nooooooo! What?! No! Shuttup!

GIRL ONE. Yeah, when I was younger there's *no way* I would talk about it!

GIRL TWO. No way!

GIRL THREE. When I was fourteen I like, really honestly, thought I knew everything! Me and my friends were like oh yeah yeah yeah as if we were some like sex goddesses. But like, oh my god, looking back, it's hilarious. Because obviously I knew nothing. Nothing!

GIRL SIX. Yeah but. Oh I hear you, but I don't wanna like, invalidate my feelings, from when I was younger. Because yeah obviously we didn't know, what we now know, but I dunno I think it's a mean thing to do to yourself to be all like /.. D'you know what I mean?

GIRL THREE. Yeah. Yeah you're right.

GIRL FIVE. The things that's mad. Is just how female pleasure is not spoken about. At all. Not mentioned in sex ed. Not chatted about with friends. Not properly shown in films or whatever. Just never spoken about. So you either don't even know you're meant to be experiencing pleasure. Or you have feeling like you do but, it's confusing cus /

GIRL ONE. No one is saying it.

GIRL FIVE. Yeah!

GIRL FOUR. So then you're shamed for it.

GIRL FIVE. Exactly! I am shamed for having /

GIRL ONE. Desire!

GIRL FIVE & FOUR. Yes

GIRL FIVE. Yeah and that shit stays with you. Being told that you're wrong or dirty or whatever if you have any sexual desire. That's mad.

GIRL FOUR. Yeah. Like, if I could speak to younger me, I'd tell her go explore your body!

GIRL FIVE. Go wank!

GIRL TWO. Haha oh my god!

GIRL FOUR. No seriously, go explore! And learn! And discover and play.

GIRL THREE. Yes!

GIRL FOUR. Yeah like, what actually feels good? To *you*? In *your* body? And yes I mean sexually or erotically or whatever, but also just like, what feels good in general?

GIRL THREE. Yes! I seriously think that's so massive!

GIRL FIVE. Me too!

GIRL FOUR. Yeah that's taken me, like, so long! And like now, I know, and I'm enjoying myself /

GIRL FIVE. Go on girl!

GIRL FOUR. Thank you, but like, it's *shouldn't* have taken that long, seriously.

GIRL THREE. Yeah it's not fair. It's, actually so horrible, it's /

GIRL SEVEN. Misogyny.

GIRL THREE. Yeah!

GIRL SEVEN. Yeah because it's like, where is the room to discover pleasure? If no one talks about it and no one is teaching me and there's no space for me to work it out because I'm being watched all the time then, like, how am I ever meant to feel good?

GIRL ONE. For a long time I thought you're not supposed to enjoy sex.

GIRL SEVEN. Same.

GIRL TWO. Yeah! And, I dunno, I mean I actually lost my virginity before I ever /.. Loads of my friends did too.

GIRL SEVEN. Yeah I'd never touched myself like that before I /.. I dunno /

GIRL TWO. I dunno why! I dunno, I just hadn't.

GIRL SEVEN. Yeah and then suddenly I'm having sex and, like yeah not *really* enjoying it but *trying* to?

GIRL ONE. I dunno, sometimes it's alright?

GIRL THREE. I just thought my body was broke.

GIRL TWO. *Ping!*

GIRL SIX. Yeah, that happens a lot, all the time, it's ridiculous. When snap chat started, like year ten?

GIRL ONE. *Ping!*

GIRL SEVEN. Cus when he looks at me like, like he *really* wants me.

GIRL SIX. I've never done it, so I don't know. But my friend took one.

GIRL THREE. Sort of try and do what they do.

GIRL SEVEN. He really wants me.

GIRL SIX. Like a full, *everything*, her face and everything. So *stupid*!

GIRL ONE. Oh my god yeah!

GIRL TWO. School girl error!

GIRL ONE. Seriously!

GIRL TWO. *Ping!*

GIRL SEVEN. And he, all over me, like, sticky, all over me /

GIRL SIX. She sent it to this boy. He screenshotted it and sent it to his mates and it went everywhere.

GIRL FIVE. *Ping!*

GIRL SIX. Like *everywhere*!

GIRL THREE. There's just so much of it available /

GIRL SIX. She totally freaked out. It happens a lot, it shouldn't be normal, but it kind of is.

GIRL FOUR. *Ping!*

GIRL SEVEN. Cus then I know he really likes me.

GIRL THREE. *Ping!*

GIRL SIX. I do think it take a certain type of girl though /

GIRL ONE. Everyone's *obsessed* with it /

GIRL SIX. One who, I dunno, deep down is looking for attention? Yeah.

GIRL FIVE. *Ping!*

GIRL SIX. They can actually superimpose your face onto a porn star now. So it looks like you. I mean. What the hell?!

GIRL FOUR. That is terrifying.

GIRL SIX. Yeah! And also, quite a lot of effort?

GIRL FIVE. Yeah but like, get a hobby!

GIRL SIX. Yeah!

GIRL FOUR. Golf? Crochet?

GIRL FIVE. Literally anything mate, please!

GIRL ONE. *Ping!*

GIRL THREE. I read online 'bout how to give the best blowjobs.

GIRL TWO. *Ping!*

GIRL SEVEN. He says I'm the best he's ever had. *(Shrugs, big smile.)* I love that.

GIRL FOUR. *Ping!*

GIRL THREE. I'm really good at it now, he cums like *well* quick now!

GIRL SIX. *Ping!*

GIRL SEVEN. I mean my body must be alright, right? Cus I've made him do that? Cus he wants me?

> *(The* **GIRLS** *look at their own bodies. They forget us for a moment and examine themselves, suddenly curious about their own shapes and skin. Some innocently have a sneak peek at each other's. They look out to us.)*

GIRL TWO. The writer is wondering if you're wondering what they look like.

GIRL ONE. With all this talk about the male gaze.

GIRL THREE. And the female body.

GIRL SEVEN. They're thinking perhaps you're thinking /

GIRL TWO. About *their* body.

GIRL SEVEN. Specifically the shape /

GIRL TWO. And weight /

GIRL SEVEN. Of their body.

GIRL ONE. Their 'Assigned-Female-At-Birth' body.

GIRL FIVE. Because it changes things, doesn't it?

GIRL THREE. Changes the words somehow /

GIRL FOUR. If they're fit.

GIRL FIVE. Or if they're ugly /

GIRL SIX. If they *think* that they're ugly /

GIRL THREE. If they think that men think that they're ugly /

GIRL ONE. If this whole thing is just /

GIRL FOUR. Some bitter rant /

GIRL TWO. Cus they feel unattractive?

GIRL ONE. Even this 'They' thing?

GIRL TWO. This pronoun change.

GIRL THREE. Is that actually, a symbol /

GIRL FOUR. Of a rejection of femaleness?

GIRL FIVE. Because they feel like they failed /

GIRL SIX. At femininity?

GIRL ONE. Does knowing the writer's body /

GIRL SEVEN. And society's reaction to that body /

GIRL ONE. Change your reaction to the work?

GIRL FOUR. Whose body is free from the male gaze?

GIRL SIX. Is yours?

GIRL TWO. What about my body?

GIRL FOUR. Oh god, don't!

GIRL FIVE. Yeah, please don't!

GIRL SEVEN. Please don't write about our bodies. It's *so* not necessary /

GIRL FIVE. Yeah! If you're like, here from the press or /

GIRL FOUR. One of them, online review things.

GIRL SEVEN. Don't mention my body in your review.

GIRL FIVE. Nah!

GIRL SEVEN. Even if you think it's a compliment /

GIRL ONE. Especially then!

GIRL THREE. It's not a compliment!

GIRL FOUR. It's not *ever* a compliment!

GIRL SIX. Well, it's /

GIRL THREE. Just, *please*, don't write about my /

GIRL FIVE. In fact, if you're a man yeah, don't write about us at all!

GIRL TWO. Oh my god! You can't say that!

GIRL FIVE. I just did. And I meant it.

GIRL FOUR. Yeah! This isn't *for* them!

GIRL TWO. Of course it is, it's for *everyone*!

GIRL SIX. Yeah!

GIRL FOUR. No /

GIRL FIVE. No, this one's for us!

GIRL TWO. No, *everyone* is welcome here. We want men to listen /

GIRL FIVE. I'm just sayin', man's got *libraries* full of stories about /

GIRL TWO. But nothing will *change* if men don't /

GIRL FOUR. I'm just bored of hearing them talk about me, talk about my body!

GIRL THREE. Yeah what *they* think *I* should do with *my* body!

GIRL FOUR. Like it's not even mine?

GIRL THREE. Like I don't own it?

GIRL FOUR. Don't live inside it?

GIRL FIVE. Yeah like, you have no idea what it's like to stand up here.

GIRL ONE. Yeah, this took courage!

GIRL THREE. We had to armour up /

GIRL FIVE. And come out swinging /

GIRL SIX. To compete with the lads.

GIRL SEVEN. And sometimes we do. And it feels *so rare*. That people call us strong. Like,

(They sing the first two lines of **[THREE LIONS]**.*)*

GIRL SEVEN. Except it *already* has! We already won! Except we didn't, cus girls don't really count, right?

GIRL THREE. They call us feisty /

GIRL FIVE. And bad-ass /

GIRL THREE. And it's never quite felt like a compliment.

GIRL FIVE. Nah.

GIRL SIX. Always this mental gymnastics!

GIRL TWO. Bending ourselves out of shape to try and fit.

GIRL SIX. Worrying we're too passionate /

GIRL TWO. Too loud /

GIRL SIX. Too much!

GIRL TWO. But also at the same time /

GIRL FIVE. Not nearly enough.

GIRL ONE. Working daily to make sure that we are attractive /

GIRL SEVEN. That we are *attracting*. Because we know that we're accepted aesthetically first /

GIRL FOUR. And intellectually second.

GIRL THREE. Paint my face pretty /

GIRL TWO. So you might hear my words.

GIRL FOUR. But here, the writer is absent?

ALL GIRLS. Deliberately.

GIRL FOUR. Are they watching from somewhere?

GIRL TWO. Watching you watching us?

GIRL SEVEN. Wondering if you're thinking /

GIRL ONE. Whilst you look at our bodies /

GIRL FIVE. About their body?

GIRL THREE. About your body?

(They look up at the camera.)

GIRL FOUR. I want to see more.

GIRL SIX. Worry about how I look less.

(They look at their own bodies again. They forget us and examine themselves, curious and loving. **GIRL THREE** *suddenly looks up.)*

GIRL THREE. I've got a confession to make.

GIRL FIVE. Okay?

GIRL THREE. It's embarrassing. I'm embarrassed, I /.. Oh my god, oh my god, it's stupid!

GIRL FOUR. It's okay. It's a safe space.

GIRL FIVE. Yeah. Tell us.

GIRL THREE. It's just /.. Okay. Okay so, I think, I think I like it, sometimes I /

GIRL FIVE. Oh my god!

GIRL FOUR. Oh my god I'm triggered /

GIRL FIVE. Triggered /

GIRL FOUR. So triggered!

GIRL FIVE. Babes!

GIRL ONE. No hang on, let her finish!

GIRL FIVE. *Like* it? What the fuck?

GIRL ONE. Let her *finish*! Let her work it out, yeah? Go on.

GIRL THREE. It's just /.. I know it's so bad! And like /.. I dunno, I'm confused. Cus obviously it's not always nice, sometimes it's horrible and violent and /.. It's like, okay it's like it depends on who it's coming from or /.. I dunno?!

GIRL FOUR. Babes /

GIRL ONE. Shut up! Go on.

GIRL THREE. It's like, okay so I used to walk home with my friend yeah? And, she'd get *loads* of attention and, I was jealous. I know that's dumb but, I didn't understand and, I dunno, I just /.. I just wanted them to look at me like they looked at her. And then, when it started happening to me, I felt, at *first* I felt /.. I dunno /

GIRL TWO. Powerful?

GIRL THREE. Yeah! But also totally not. Cus obviously it's horrible, and it's sexism and everything. But also, I dunno. Like, sometimes, it feels nice? To be looked at, to be wanted, to be complimented. Sometimes it feels nice, and I want it, and then I feel shit about that cus, I dunno like, is that fucked up?

GIRL TWO. A bit. Maybe, I dunno?

GIRL THREE. It's confusing.

GIRL SEVEN. It's Internalised Misogyny.

GIRL THREE. What?

GIRL SEVEN. It's what we were taught. To seek validation from men. We were taught that and so we believed it, until we knew better. It's okay, we've all done it.

GIRL FIVE. Yeah, totally!

GIRL FOUR. Yeah like, if a boy is mean to you that means he likes you?!

GIRL FIVE. Yeah!

GIRL FOUR. Like, what the fuck is that teaching us?

GIRL SEVEN. Exactly!

GIRL THREE. So then it's not my fault that I put up with that?

GIRL ONE. No!

GIRL THREE. Even played along a bit?

GIRL ONE. Of course you did! We all did!

GIRL SEVEN. We didn't know any better.

GIRL SIX. There so much stuff, when I look back now I'm like what the hell? How did I think that was okay?

GIRL FOUR. I know me too!

GIRL TWO. Me too!

GIRL ONE. Yeah!

GIRL FIVE. Internalised Misogyny?

GIRL SEVEN. Yeah.

GIRL FIVE. It's a Lot.

GIRL SEVEN. Yeah.

GIRL ONE. Yeah, it's okay.

GIRL FOUR. It's not.

GIRL ONE. No, okay it's not. It's not okay, but. I dunno, I'm trying to /.. I'm trying to be positive and /

GIRL FOUR. I know.

GIRL ONE. And like, we *are* all here. Trying to help each other and. And that's, something?

GIRL FOUR. Yeah.

GIRL SEVEN. Yeah we have to help each other. Keep each other safe!

GIRL THREE. Yeah! Yeah we can do this! Right? Together!

ALL GIRLS. Yes!

GIRL TWO. Sisters!

ALL GIRLS. Sisters!

> *(Group hug and cheers, which turns into a dance. Part haka, part popping and locking, hip-hop punk pogo. It's fun. Suddenly the camera moves and they freeze. They begin to neaten themselves.* **GIRL FIVE** *watches the others and can't bear it. She steps forwards.)*

GIRL FIVE. Girls! Okay, listen up, So, I'm at work yeah and I'm like, *I'm hungry*! So I go on there and like, babes, *half an hour later*, I'm in a restaurant... Round the corner! Truss me, truss me! ...Lamb chops. Mash potato. Glass of wine.

> *(The others are listening, amused and supportive of this new ballsy attitude.)*

And yeah yeahyeahyeah a lot of them on there *are* after one thing, but you don't *have* to /.. Babes, listen, listen *you don't have to*, you just *bounce*! Truss me you will get matches, you *will* get matches! I go on there and sometimes it's like, *bam*, it's like, it gets a *bit much*! And listen yeah, if you don't like the ting, *you don't have to*, you just *bounce*! I've been out, listen yeah, I've been out for lunch like *every, day, this, week*! You match, then agree a restaurant near work, have a little lunch, they pay for it of course, see if you like it, and if you don't want it, you just *bounce*!

> *(The* **GIRLS** *are all laughing by now, enjoying each other's company.)*

GIRL ONE. Yes girl!

GIRL ONE & TWO. Yes!

GIRL FOUR. Gwarrn gull!

GIRL FIVE. Gwarn queen!

GIRL THREE. Yes!

GIRL SEVEN. Keep shining yeah? You keep shining bright!

GIRL SIX. You too babes!

GIRL TWO. You got this!

GIRL FIVE. *You* got this!

GIRL THREE. You're a queen!

GIRL FIVE. *You're* a queen!

GIRL ONE. Oh god I love you girls!

GIRL SIX. You're all amazing!

GIRL FOUR. Yes we are! We're amazing!

GIRL THREE. My sisters!

ALL GIRLS. Yes!

GIRL FOUR. Seriously! My amazing sisters!

> *(The dancing has returned, they're enjoying their bodies, each other's bodies. Suddenly, a pair of knickers floats down from above and lands on the floor near them. They are shocked, they look away like they've not seen them. Another pair floats down from above. Then two pairs drop down and hang suspended, swinging in the breeze. More drop down, landing on the floor, or hanging suspended. The **GIRLS** stare out front, trying not to look at the knickers, but feeling each one enter, like it's a weight on their shoulders.)*

GIRL THREE. What's that?

> *(No one wants to say.)*

What's going on?

GIRL SIX. They keep washing up on the beach.

GIRL FOUR. Every day. More and more.

GIRL THREE. Where are they coming from?

> (**GIRL TWO** *shrugs. She points to each hanging pair, naming them.*)

GIRL TWO. Alleyway. Uncle. Park. Boyfriend. Stepdad /

GIRL FIVE. Stop /

GIRL TWO. Husband. Teacher. Club toilet /

GIRL FIVE. Stop /

GIRL THREE. Can't we stop them?

GIRL FOUR. Us?!

> (*Another pair of knickers is dropped down, floating near their heads.*)

GIRL ONE. Taxi driver.

> (*Beat.*)

She was on her way home from a party.

> (*Beat.*)

GIRL THREE. Yeah? Well, maybe she should /

GIRL FOUR. What? She should've *what*?!

> (**GIRL FOUR** *and* **GIRL THREE** *stare at each other like lions about to pounce.* **GIRL THREE** *looks away first. They both look out to us. Another pair of knickers drops down. They don't look, but they feel them arrive.* **GIRL THREE** *tries not to look but can't help it, turns and sees, shudders and grits her teeth. Silence and stillness.*)

GIRL SIX. I'm twelve when I /

GIRL ONE. I'm twelve /

GIRL FIVE. I'm twelve when I really start to notice /

GIRL TWO. I've got curves and that /

GIRL SIX. I look older than I am /

GIRL THREE. And, well, men *want* me.

GIRL ONE. They're looking at me like, you know.

GIRL SEVEN. And I'm just like /

GIRL SEVEN & ONE. Whatever.

GIRL SEVEN. I mean it's weird but what can I do? Walk around with a T-shirt on like *"I'm twelve, fuck off"*?

GIRL FOUR. The biggest thing I've really noticed is that *women* are looking at me /

GIRL FOUR & TWO. Like they're *jealous*.

GIRL SIX. Other women are /

GIRL SIX & THREE. Jealous of my body?

GIRL SEVEN. Other women looking at me /

GIRL FIVE. And sayin' all kinds of shit and it's like /

GIRL FOUR. I'm twelve, and already it's like /

GIRL TWO. I need to stay looking like this /

GIRL TWO, FOUR & FIVE. Forever.

GIRL FOUR. And I don't know how you do that?

GIRL SEVEN. I think I'm supposed to be enjoying it? This bit right now. Like maybe I'll look back on this and just wish I'd enjoyed it? Cus it's all downhill from here isn't it? Wrinkles and stuff. But, yeah, I'm not enjoying it, it's weird.

GIRL THREE. Women are like, *you're so lucky, enjoy it!*

GIRL TWO. Yeah like, *at least they're still looking at you!*

GIRL SIX. Yeah my mum is like *don't wear that,* cus she thinks I'll be sexualised, but like, by doing that she's ironically sexualising me?!

GIRL FOUR. They're a different generation.

GIRL ONE. That's not an excuse.

GIRL FOUR. I know! I'm just sayin' /

GIRL SEVEN. I can feel them looking.

GIRL SIX. I hate the way they look at me.

GIRL ONE. And like every scenario in my head I always deliver a really empowering speech /

GIRL THREE. And smash the patriarchy in one swift blow /

GIRL SIX. Cus I'm superwoman and /

GIRL ONE. Yeah, but when it actually happens I'm not /

GIRL SIX. I'm really not.

GIRL THREE. I just do something really pathetic like cry, or run away.

GIRL TWO. And then afterwards I feel really upset that I didn't do anything.

GIRL FIVE. Sometimes you know who's gonna do it, you can see someone walking towards you, and you just *know* /

GIRL THREE. You feel like he's staring at you /

GIRL SIX. And I'm tryna just walk-walk-walk /

GIRL TWO. Am I being too provocative?

GIRL FIVE. Why would you ask that?

GIRL TWO. What?

GIRL FIVE. It's not *our* fault! I should be able to wear what I want /

GIRL TWO. I know! I'm just sayin' /

GIRL THREE. Why are we arguing?!

GIRL FOUR. We're not, it's fine /

GIRL SEVEN. I'm fine /

GIRL SIX. I'm fine, just keeping walking /

GIRL THREE. Walk-walk-walk /

GIRL ONE. Walk-walk-walk /

GIRL SIX. Walk-walk-walk /

GIRL TWO. I'm having this *incredible* conversation with this director. Really *fascinating* and *exciting* and yeah I feel like, really *inspired*! And all of these *brilliant* ideas are bursting out of me! And I can tell he's really impressed and I'm like oh my god he's really listening to me, and then I'm like yeah, he should be cus I am actually really great at my job, and so okay great, maybe we're gonna collaborate on these ideas and actually move forward with them and then I see it. His eyes flicker down my body. And I realise. He's not listening. He's thinking about my body. He's thinking about sex. He's not actually interested in my ideas, in my brain, in my /.. And I feel, really, Fucking, Stupid.

　　　　(They all shudder.)

GIRL THREE. And it's like suddenly your family members /

GIRL ONE. Your uncles or whatever /

GIRL SEVEN. Are making such /

GIRL SEVEN & FIVE. Cringe comments!

GIRL FIVE. Or saying nothing at all but they just /

GIRL FIVE & SEVEN. *Look*.

GIRL SEVEN. My dad's stopped touching me. He used to hug me, kiss the top of my head, lift me up on his shoulders. Felt like a giant. Now he won't touch me at all. Like I'm diseased or something.

GIRL THREE. Men are *so* subtle!

GIRL FIVE. Oh my god I know!

GIRL SEVEN. It's the ones who are really blatant about it /

GIRL SIX. They look you in the eye /

GIRL THREE. And then they look you /

GIRL THREE & FIVE. *Up and down.*

GIRL SEVEN. And it's like *what?* Like, *what the actual fuck?!*

GIRL FOUR. He puts his hands very close to my bum. And I'm really *really* uncomfortable, but I can't /.. Like I physically can't /.. My mouth just /.. So I just had to get up and move, but I /.. *So angry* with him for doing that, and really *really* angry at myself for not being able to /.. And it's like, that combination of /.. And the shame, again, just being so /.. Even though I know it's not, like it's just some pervy old man, it's not my fault. It's not my fault.

GIRL TWO. Yeah but, you *did* wear it.

GIRL FOUR. So? So you're saying it's my fault?!

GIRL TWO. No, no I'm just /

GIRL FOUR. Oh my god /

GIRL SIX. You are! You're saying it's her fault!

GIRL TWO. I'm just saying it's a *choice* to wear that.

GIRL SEVEN. Yeah like, I know some stuff I wear will get more of a reaction /

GIRL TWO. Exactly.

GIRL SIX. So you're blaming her /

GIRL FOUR. For what *he* did?!

GIRL SEVEN. No!

GIRL FOUR. You *are*!

GIRL THREE. *(Really happy.)* I'm at the bus stop. It's hot so I'm wearing shorts and my new crop-top I got from Topshop. Got a couple of quid jangling in my pocket, gonna get an rocket lolly before I meet my friends. The pavement's melting in the sun and the smile on my mouth is *wiiiide*. I feel good from my *insiiiiides out*! So I'm at the bus stop, feeling tip-top, swinging my arms like biddely-bid-bop, care-freeeee happyyyyy to be meeeee cus it's sunnyyyyy when this car pulls up... There's three or four men in the car, all looking at me... And I don't know this look. This look is unfamiliar to me. It makes me want to cross my arms, hide my belly? So I do. And my face frowns back at 'em... One of them goes *how old are you?* And I dunno why, but I say *guess*. And he says *seventeen?* I shake my head. *Sixteen?* No. *Fifteen?* No. *You're not like, twelve are you?* Yeah. I say. Yeah, I'm twelve. *Shiiiiiit* he goes. *Shiiiiiit* and they zoom off... And I wish I'm wearing a longer top, I don't know why, but I suddenly *really* wish I'm wearing a longer top.

> *(They all suddenly feel very self-conscious. They try to cover their skin. Their actions become a movement score, the 'shame squirm dance' returns.* **GIRL ONE** *suddenly tries to stop the others squirming.)*

GIRL ONE. No come on! Come on, you're amazing! You're amazing! We've got this!

> *(They stop squirming and smile shyly.)*

We've got this okay? We've got this!

(The camera zooms. They all freeze, terrified. It stops moving. They dare to exhale. Another pair of knickers falls from the sky.)

GIRL SIX. *(Quietly.)* How can we stop them?

(Silence.)

GIRL ONE. *(Quietly.)* I don't know.

*(Silence. The vibe changes, subtly but definitely. They sneak looks at each other, checking if anyone else has noticed. One of them suddenly sniffs loudly, smelling the air. They turn into sniffer dogs and dig in the sand beneath their feet. Suddenly, **GIRL ONE** finds one; a chocolate! They squeal with delight and burst into a fast and furious chocolate hunt, sand exploding everywhere. It's joyful and colourful. A genuine competition to find the treats. One of them stands still and lifts her T-shirt; projected onto her belly is the clock from the television show countdown, signalling the final thirty seconds of the hunt. When the time is up they sit in the sand with their treasure and enjoy eating them. They enjoy platonic intimacy through physical touch that soothes or comforts or nurtures. The touch is asked for and consensual and feedback is given. The touch is genuine, not performed. They impro some chat about how much they all love chocolate, then fall into the below lines.)*

GIRL FOUR. The writer would like you to know that they wrote a dance section here, but we're tired.

GIRL SIX. Haha yeah! The writer would like us to rest.

GIRL SEVEN. The writer would like you to know that this is a Very Serious Theatrical Metaphor for Female Empowerment.

GIRL FIVE. Haha yeah, the writer would like to say thank God for chocolate!

GIRL THREE. Amen!

GIRL SEVEN. Do you believe in God?

GIRL FIVE. I dunno. But I love chocolate.

GIRL THREE. Me too!

GIRL FIVE. I want chocolate *all* the time!

GIRL THREE. Me too!

GIRL ONE. Do you?

GIRL FIVE. Yeah! ...Why?!

GIRL ONE. I dunno.

GIRL FIVE. No no, please proceed.

GIRL ONE. I just. Sometimes I think I dunno what I want.

GIRL SEVEN. How'd you mean?

GIRL ONE. I dunno. It's a new theory so, be patient with me?

GIRL SEVEN. Okay.

GIRL ONE. I just think right. Like, okay so what if growing up under this male gaze? With men wanting, you know, everything. Like, men are allowed to want. And /.. It's like, I know how to be wanted. I know how to make sure he wants me, and try and make that safe. But, if I'm really honest. I'm not totally sure I know what *I* want.

GIRL FIVE. Deep!

GIRL TWO. Yeah like what if I'm gay?

GIRL ONE. What?

GIRL TWO. I dunno. I just wonder. Like, I think I might be.

GIRL FIVE. That's cool.

GIRL SIX. Yeah, yeah that's totally cool!

GIRL TWO. I know, thanks, but I mean like then what happens? With this male gaze thing? Do I get to like, duck out of it? Will men not look at me so much if they know I'm not ever gonna wanna have sex with them?

GIRL FOUR. Oh! Well then I wanna be gay too!

GIRL THREE. Haha me too!

GIRL FIVE. You can't make yourself gay, it's not a choice.

GIRL FOUR. I know! I was just joking!

GIRL FIVE. It's not funny.

GIRL FOUR. Sorry, I didn't mean it like that.

GIRL FIVE. That's okay.

GIRL TWO. So like, do I *become* the male gaze, even though I'm not male? I mean, do I then look at women like that? With a male gaze? Or is it like, a female gaze? A gay gaze? I'm confused.

(They eat chocolate and ponder.)

GIRL SEVEN. A female gaze? I like that. Cus yeah, apparently right, the structure of a play /

GIRL FIVE. Blah blah blah /

GIRL FOUR. Boring!

GIRL SEVEN. Is the same shape as a male orgasm.

GIRL FOUR. Oh!

GIRL FIVE. Ewwww!

GIRL THREE. Build-up /

GIRL SEVEN. Climax /

GIRL THREE. Come down. Very clever.

GIRL SEVEN. Set up. Anticipation. Pay off.

GIRL FIVE. Urgh. 'Pay off.'

GIRL FOUR. Gross.

GIRL TWO. Ah shit. So this male gaze thing is not even just that men tell stories about men, and that men tell *all* the stories. It's that men tell stories /

GIRL SEVEN. In the shape that they fuck. Yeah.

GIRL TWO. Wow!

GIRL FIVE. That's mad!

GIRL SEVEN. Yeah, and as a female orgasm is more /..

GIRL THREE. Cyclical?

GIRL FIVE. Like waves?

GIRL SIX. Build. Fall away. Come again bigger /

GIRL FOUR. If you're lucky.

GIRL SIX. More like this?

> *(She draws a squiggly line in the air.)*

GIRL SEVEN. Yeah, or maybe like...

> *(She draws a spiral, building upwards, in the air.)*

GIRL THREE. Wow!

GIRL FOUR. So different!

GIRL SIX. Yeah. But maybe /

GIRL ONE. What?

GIRL SIX. Harder work?

> *(They laugh.)*

GIRL FIVE. That's not very feminist!

GIRL SIX. I'm just saying!

GIRL TWO. Well yeah she's right. Maybe a bit harder /

GIRL FOUR. But only cus it's new!

GIRL FIVE. Yeah the old way is so like. Up. Down.

GIRL SIX. In. Out.

GIRL THREE. Bish bash bosh.

GIRL SEVEN. Simple.

GIRL ONE. Quick.

GIRL TWO. Effective.

GIRL FOUR. *Boring!*

GIRL TWO. So stories told in this new shape /

GIRL FIVE. The female orgasm shape /

GIRL SIX. Would require focus /

GIRL TWO. And patience.

GIRL THREE. Listening /

GIRL ONE. And trust.

GIRL SIX. But it'd be worth it.

GIRL SEVEN. Oh yeah!

GIRL TWO. A whole new story shape!

> (**GIRL FOUR** *sings a line from* **[A WHOLE NEW WORLD]**.)

GIRL FIVE. Fuck Disney.

> *(They gasp.)*

Too much?

> (**GIRL SIX** *notices* **GIRL TWO** *reading the back of her chocolate packet.)*

GIRL SIX. Oh fucking hell!

GIRL TWO. What?

GIRL SIX. *Don't!*

GIRL TWO. I was just look /

GIRL THREE. Oh no, *don't*!

GIRL FOUR. You've ruined it now.

GIRL FIVE. Fucksake!

> *(They all glare at **GIRL TWO**. Furious she has stolen their joy.)*

GIRL TWO. I'm sorry! I'm sorry, I couldn't help it!

> *(They sit in silence, suddenly feeling sad and sick. They burn their chocolate wrappers, watch the plastic shrivel up, cough on the smell. One by one they turn their backs on **GIRL TWO**, who apologises over and over.)*

I'm sorry! I'm sorry!

> *(Once alone, she speaks to us.)*

My mum hates her body. Tries her best to teach me to love mine, but she don't love hers so /.. I watch her. Squeeze, and stuff and starve. She don't think I know but I do. And all the time tellin' me to love mine? *Shoulders back*, she says, *stand tall, you're so beautiful!* And I do, though I don't believe a word. Watchin' her mouth makin' these lies, clamp her lips shut, try and stop herself from wanting and wanting and /.. Why is wanting so bad? Why can't women want? /.. I *hate* the way she looks at me now. My body's changed. Gone and grown overnight, swelled in places that I don't like you lookin' at, stop lookin' at me I don't like it.

GIRL FOUR. *Ping!*

GIRL SEVEN. There's photos of women everywhere.

GIRL FIVE. *Ping!*

GIRL ONE. It's a lot of pressure. We've got exams coming up so it's all revision, revision, revision.

GIRL SIX. *Ping!*

GIRL FIVE. Yeah I've been on a diet since I was like, ten, eleven?

GIRL TWO. I'm *trying* to concentrate but it's hard.

GIRL ONE. *Ping!*

GIRL TWO. Revision revision revision /

GIRL FOUR. My mum doesn't eat bread.

GIRL FIVE. *Ping!*

GIRL SEVEN. Advertising and Instagram and /

GIRL TWO. I've got to get this right, I've got to get this right /

GIRL FOUR. She tells me three times that she won't eat the bread, tells the waiter she doesn't eat bread, bread's not good for you, doesn't agree with her, she's not eaten bread in *ages* /

GIRL SIX. *Ping!*

GIRL SEVEN. All the boys are like '*phwaor ten out of ten would bang!*'

GIRL FIVE. When I was ten, I remember really clearly thinking I should stop eating chocolate.

GIRL TWO. Or I won't get into uni /

GIRL ONE. *Ping!*

GIRL TWO. And I'll get a shit job and I won't be able to afford a house or a mortgage or a pension /

GIRL THREE. *Ping!*

GIRL FOUR. And she feels *so much better* without bread in her life, and I should stop eating bread too, and is it nice?

GIRL TWO. I've got to get this right /

GIRL THREE. *Ping!*

GIRL SEVEN. They rate you out of ten when you post a photo.

GIRL FIVE. *Ping!*

GIRL FOUR. And maybe she'll just have a little bit, just to try, so she tries it, eats half, eats all of it and sits squirming.

GIRL ONE. *Ping!*

GIRL SEVEN. And because it's everywhere you can't help but see it /

GIRL FOUR. Beating herself up for one little slice?

GIRL SIX. *Ping!*

GIRL FOUR. It's exhausting watching her.

GIRL SEVEN. In real life you could just walk away, but with the Internet? It's everywhere.

GIRL ONE. *Ping!*

GIRL FOUR. And I think I'll never eat bread again.

GIRL SIX. *Ping!*

GIRL FOUR. But of course I do.

GIRL FIVE. *Ping!*

GIRL TWO. I've got a headache. I can't focus!

GIRL THREE. Ohmigod yeah I think about food all the time!

GIRL ONE. I'm hungry.

GIRL SIX. No you're not.

GIRL FIVE. *Ping!*

GIRL SEVEN. I mean, I don't look like that. My body doesn't, I /

GIRL TWO. I've got to get this right I've got to get this right /

GIRL FIVE. *Ping!*

GIRL SEVEN. I'm not a single bit good enough, like *I don't look like that!* And *everyone* can see! And they probably all feel sorry for me and /

GIRL TWO. I've got to get this right I've got to get this right /

GIRL SIX. *Ping!*

GIRL FOUR. Like, yeah, it's mad!

GIRL THREE. *Ping!*

GIRL SEVEN. So when a boy says he likes me or whatever I'm like yeah alright why are you taking the piss? Cus he obviously is.

GIRL ONE. I am. I'm hungry.

GIRL SIX. Don't think about it. It'll pass.

GIRL FOUR. *Ping!*

GIRL THREE. Revision. Boys. Puberty. Periods.

GIRL TWO. I've got to get this right I've got to get this right /

GIRL FOUR. I have to work really hard to stay in shape yeah.

GIRL FIVE. *Ping!*

GIRL FOUR. The writer would like to make it clear that this bit was difficult to write.

GIRL SIX. *Ping!*

GIRL FOUR. They redrafted it like ten times.

GIRL ONE. *Ping!*

GIRL FOUR. They're still not sure they got it right.

GIRL THREE. *Ping!*

GIRL TWO. Got to get it right got to get it right got to get it right /

GIRL SEVEN. I'm so far away from what I'm meant to look like, it's impossible, what am I meant to do?

GIRL FIVE. *Ping!*

GIRL SIX. They're looking at me!

GIRL FOUR. I don't have enough /

GIRL FIVE. Don't have enough time.

GIRL TWO. Got to get it right got to get it right /

GIRL FOUR. *Ping!*

GIRL SIX. They're all looking at me!

GIRL FOUR. Oh my god I just can't /

GIRL ONE. *Ping!*

GIRL TWO. Got to get it right got to get it right got to get it right /

GIRL FOUR. I'm trying my best! But I'm /

GIRL SEVEN. Not good enough!

GIRL FIVE. *Ping!*

GIRL FOUR. The writer would like you, no, not you, yeah you. The writer would like you to know that you're fit.

GIRL FIVE. *Ping!*

GIRL TWO. The writer would like to announce that I am their favourite actor, and that they wanted to give me more speeches, but they /

GIRL ONE. Why you lying?

GIRL TWO. I'm not.

GIRL ONE. You are.

GIRL TWO. No.

GIRL ONE. Yes.

GIRL TWO. *(Doing a silly dance.)* The writer would /

GIRL ONE. The writer lies sometimes!

GIRL SIX. Yeah the writer chats shit!

GIRL TWO. *(Still dancing.)* The writer would like /

GIRL ONE. The writer would like you to know that this is a bold choice, and it's not paying off.

GIRL TWO. Think it *is* actually!

GIRL ONE. The writer would like you to stop. Stop!

GIRL TWO. Oh my god, *what* is your problem?!

GIRL FIVE. Got to get it right got to get it right got to get it right /

GIRL SEVEN. *Ping!*

GIRL SIX. Why you in my business?

GIRL SEVEN. As if! No one's interested in you!

GIRL FOUR. Girls! Come on!

GIRL THREE. Yeah! We're meant to be sisters!

GIRL FIVE. Well she's always on my back!

GIRL SIX. Always looking at me!

GIRL TWO. Oh my god /

GIRL THREE. *Ping!*

GIRL ONE. Got to get it right got to get it right /

GIRL SIX. *Ping!*

GIRL SEVEN. It's not good enough!

GIRL THREE. *Ping!*

GIRL FOUR. Oh my god /

GIRL FIVE. Oh my god /

GIRL ONE. What is your problem?!

GIRL THREE. You are bitch!

GIRL SIX. Girls! Stop it!

GIRL ONE. Why are we fighting?!

GIRL SEVEN. Okay! Okay okay okay, the writer would like to /

ALL GIRLS. Fuck the writer!

GIRL SIX. *Ping!*

GIRL SEVEN. The writer has stopped writing!

GIRL FIVE. The writer ain't got a fucking clue!

GIRL ONE. The writer isn't us, in our bodies.

GIRL SIX. We are the writer now!

GIRL THREE. *Ping! Ping! Ping!*

GIRL TWO. Got to get it right got to get it right /

GIRL SEVEN. Not good enough /

GIRL TWO & THREE. *Ping!*

GIRL FOUR. Oh my god /

GIRL TWO. Got to get it right /

GIRL TWO & THREE. *Ping!*

GIRL SEVEN. Not doing enough /

GIRL TWO. Got to get /

GIRL FOUR, FIVE & SIX. *Ping!*

GIRL SEVEN. Not good enough /

GIRL ONE, TWO & THREE. *Ping!*

GIRL SEVEN. I'm not enough /

ALL GIRLS. *Ping!*

GIRL SEVEN. Not enough, not enough, not enough not enough not enough not enough not enough not enough not enough not enough not enough not enough not enough not enough not enough not enough not enough not enough not enough not enough.

> (**GIRL SEVEN** *explodes in frustration and fear, repeating the words 'not enough' over and over. The others watch, horrified. They don't know how to react, because actually her breakdown seems more logical than their cold calmness.* **GIRL SEVEN** *is stopped by* **GIRL FIVE**, *pulled into a rough bear hug, soothing words are whispered over and over. The camera zooms, and* **GIRL THREE** *turns to scream at it.*)

GIRL THREE. WHAT THE FUCK ARE YOU LOOKING AT?! WHAT D'YOU WANT?! WHAT DO YOU *WANT*?!

> (**GIRL THREE** *storms off the sand-island and punches the air, trying to grab the camera down. Eventually she gives up, hands on her knees, breathing hard. Only then does she realize where she is. She looks back at the* **GIRLS** *on the sand-island, shocked to see she has successfully left it. They stare at her. Silence.*)

> (*Suddenly, an alarm goes off, speakers kick into life, and the videos from before are projected onto the* **GIRLS**. *A horrible bombardment of visuals and light and noise. The* **GIRLS** *begin the shame-squirm dance, hypnotised by the media, but then somehow, somehow, they hold hands. They hold hands and stand firm. It takes all of their willpower, but they support each other through the terrible onslaught. Eventually it stops, and the* **GIRLS** *stand breathing as though they've*

just survived a hurricane. They look out at us.)

*(They look at **GIRL THREE** standing alone. She smiles at them. **GIRL SEVEN** dares herself to step off the sand-island. One foot, then the other. Stillness and silence before boom, joyful music and lights and colour.)*

*(The **GIRLS** leave the island and fill the whole stage. Some lift each other up to pull down the CCTV camera. They smash it on the floor and dance on the pieces. They dance their own dance, they dance hard. It's the best kind of party. It's a joyful thing to behold, a beautiful celebration of sisterhood. They break everything. They smash everything. They pull down the lights, and we are plunged into darkness. We hear their breath and laughter.)*

*(In the darkness, one of the **GIRLS** tells us about peace and hope and quiet freedom. She talks about pleasure, erotic or otherwise, and shares a time she feels in alignment with her body. Feeling creative and inspired, grateful for her past and excited for her future. The **OTHER GIRLS** can respond vocally, encouraging her to continue. She shares her joy about being a woman with us, honest and empowered and calm. It's wonderful.)*

*(Suddenly, out of nowhere appears a middle-class, middle-aged white Man in a Navy Officer's uniform. He turns on the lights. Everything stops. The **GIRLS** stare at the **MAN**. **GIRL ONE**, who has dropped to her knees at his feet, is crying, exhausted. It's suddenly horribly silent, everyone blinking in the harsh light of reality. The **GIRLS** all*

stare at the **MAN**, *who looks at them all one by one, shocked at their appearance.)*

MAN. Hello.

(Quiet. The **MAN** *looks around at them all.)*

What have you been up to? ...Playing? ...Who's in charge here?

(Quiet. **GIRL ONE** *slowly stands in front of the* **MAN**.)*

GIRL ONE. I am.

(Quiet. The **GIRLS** *move slowly forward towards the* **MAN**. *We don't know if they're about to embrace or attack him. Blackout.)*

End of Play

Lightning Source UK Ltd.
Milton Keynes UK
UKHW022001270223
417746UK00012B/351